GREEKS IN PTOLEMAIC EGYPT

American Society of Papyrologists
CLASSICS IN PAPYROLOGY

*

Volume 1
Life in Egypt under Roman Rule
by Naphtali Lewis

*

Volume 2
Greeks in Ptolemaic Egypt
by Naphtali Lewis

GREEKS IN PTOLEMAIC EGYPT

*Case Studies in the
Social History of the
Hellenistic World*

NAPHTALI LEWIS

AMERICAN SOCIETY OF PAPYROLOGISTS
OAKVILLE, CONNECTICUT

Published by
the American Society of Papyrologists
at The David Brown Book Company
P O Box 511, Oakville, CT 06779, USA

Reprinted from the original Oxford University Press
edition of 1986.

Library of Congress Cataloging-in-Publication Data

Lewis, Naphtali.
    Greeks in ptolemaic Egypt / by Naphtali Lewis.
        p. cm. -- (Classics in papyrology ; v. 2)
    Includes index.
    ISBN 0-9700591-2-4 (pbk. : alk. paper)
    1. Greeks--Egypt. 2. Egypt--Civilization--332 B.C.-638 A.D. I. Title. II. Series.

    DT72.G7 L49 2001
    932'.02--dc21

                                                            2001022491

Printed in Great Britain
at the Short Run Press, Exeter
on acid-free paper

To

JEAN BINGEN

Professeur à l'Université de Bruxelles

in friendship and admiration

Contents

Maps

Plates

Prefatory Notes

The Ptolemaic Dynasty

(The Roman numerals are a modern convention, employed for convenience in distinguishing the different Ptolemies in the sequence.)

Rulers	*Dates of rule (BC)*
Ptolemy I Soter	305–283
II Philadelphos	285–246
III Euergetes	246–222
IV Philopator	222–204
V Epiphanes	204–181
VI Philometor	181–145
VII Eupator	145
VIII Euergetes II (*'physkon'*)	145–116 (ruler in Cyrene 163–145)
IX Soter II (*'lathyros'*)	116–107, 88–80 (ruler in Cyprus 107–88)
X Alexandros	107–88 (ruler in Cyprus before 107)
XI Alexandros II	80
XII Neos Dionysos (*'aulētēs'*)	80–58, 55–51
*Berenikē	58–55
*Ptolemy XIII	51–47
*Kleopatra VII Thea Philopator	51–30
*Ptolemy XIV	47–44
Ptolemy XV Caesarion	44–30

*children of Ptolemy XII

THE EPITHETS

adelphoi: 'siblings'
aulētēs: 'flute player'
† *Caesarion:* 'little Caesar'
dikaiosynē: 'justice (incarnate)
epiphanēs: '(god) manifest'
euergetēs (fem. *-tis*): 'benefactor, -tress'

eupatōr: 'of noble father'
lathyros: 'chickling'
neos Dionysos: 'the new (god) Dionysos'
nikēphoros: 'victorious'
philadelphos: 'brother-loving, sister-loving'

† Modern scholarship generally accepts Kleopatra's assertion that he was her son by Julius Caesar.

philomētōr: 'mother-loving'   *sōtēr:* (fem. *-teira*): 'saviour'
philopatōr: 'father-loving'   *thea:* 'goddess'
physkōn: 'pot-belly'

The Calendar

Years. These were counted in sequence for each reigning monarch.
The first year began with the ruler's accession (real or claimed), the
second in the following autumn on the New Year's Day (Thoth 1)
of the Egyptian calendar.

Months and days. The Ptolemaic dynasty brought with it the Macedonian lunar calendar. After several decades of separate computa-
tion, the twelve months of that calendar were equated with those of
the Egyptian solar calendar with which they approximately coincided
at the time. That equation remained fixed thereafter, but for ordinary everyday purposes, and even in official documents, the names of
the Macedonian months came to be used less and less. The sequence
of the Egyptian months, each of thirty days, was as follows:

Thōth	Phamenōth
Phaōphi	Pharmouthi
Hathyr	Pachōn
Choiak	Payni
Tybi	Ep(e)iph
Mech(e)ir	Mesorē

After the twelve months, totalling 360 days, came five intercalary
days, called in Greek *epagomenai*, 'added on'. No provision was made
for what we call leap year. As a result, Ptolemaic dates shift by one
day every four years when translated into the reckoning of our own
calendar. Thus, Thoth 1 corresponds to 27 October for 261–258 BC,
to 26 October for the years 257–254, to 25 October for 253–250, and
so on down the line.

Conversion. In this book our calendar's equivalents of the Egyptian
dates are given wherever possible. Where only the Ptolemaic year is
known, as that year ran from autumn to autumn, it will be shown as
203/2, 146/5 etc.

Spelling and Pronunciation

Personal and place-names are written in this book in accordance
with today's increasing practice of transliterating the Greek spelling

in preference to Latinizing the forms as has been done since the Renaissance, following the practice of the Romans themselves. Thus we now write Lysandros rather than Lysander, Kleopatra rather than Cleopatra, and so on. Excepted, however, are those few instances where the Latin or Anglicized spelling is so deeply ingrained in current usage as to render change gratuitous: thus we will write Alexander the Great, and Ptolemy for a ruler of the dynasty, but Alexandros and Ptolemaios for ordinary wights bearing those names.

Unlike the chaotic situation that is often the despair of foreigners learning English, the ancient languages had but a single sound for each of their vowels and consonants. The vowels and two unfamiliar (to us) consonants were sounded approximately as follows:

a as in English *aha*	ō as in *over*
e as in *get*	y as in *syntax*
ē as in *prey*	ai as in *aisle*
i as in *it*	ou as in *ghoul*
ī as in *machine*	kh as in German *ach*
o as in *come*	ch similarly but more lightly aspirated

In this book long vowels will normally be indicated only when a name or epithet first occurs in a chapter or document, but will be shown consistently where needed for clarity, as for example, in Totoēs, to remind the reader that the last four letters sound as two syllables and not like the English word 'toes'.

Abbreviations

The source material for this book consists of some 600 papyri (about forty of them in the Egyptian script that we call Demotic, the rest in Greek), supplemented by a few ostraca. In citing one or another of these sources the convention is to use *P.* for papyrus and *O.* for ostracon, followed by an identifying abbreviation, usually either the site where the papyrus or ostracon was found, as in *P. Teb.* (tynis), or the name of the finder or purchaser, as in *P. Grenf.* (ell), or the present location of the collection, as in *P. Lond.* (on). The principal exceptions to this convention encountered in this book are:

BGU for the Greek documentary papyri ('*U*rkunden') in the Egyptian Museums of *B*erlin, East and West.
P. Ent. for the collected petitions (*enteuxeis* in Greek) of Chapter 4.
UPZ for U. Wilcken's monumental re-edition of the Serapeion documents of Chapter 5.

PSI = *Papiri greci e latini* (Florence, 1912–).
WO = U. Wilcken, *Griechische Ostraka aus Aegypten und Nubien*, 2 vols.
(Leipzig and Berlin, 1899. Reprinted with addenda Amsterdam, 1970).

The following abbreviations are also used in the Notes:

SB = *Sammelbuch griechischer Urkunden aus Aegypten*, 1913– , a continuing series in which are reprinted documents published in journals, occasional volumes, etc.
SEG = *Supplementum Epigraphicum Graecum* (Leiden, 1923–).

Convenient lists of all the principal publications, with their abbreviations, are available in the following:

J. F. Oates *et al.*, *Checklist of Editions of Greek Papyri and Ostraca, Bulletin of the American Society of Papyrologists*, Supplement 4 (1985).
E. G. Turner, *Greek Papyri. An Introduction* (Oxford, 1968), second (paperback) edition, 1980, pp. 156–71.

Introduction

Greek history, as taught in our schools and colleges, typically comes to a close in 338 BC, when Philip of Macedon ended the independence of the city-states; sometimes the course syllabus goes on for another fifteen years, to the death of Alexander the Great. These limits are determined by a rationale which sees no point in studying the political institutions of the city-states after their heyday, and deplores the way in which the glorious culture of the Greeks lost its clear identity when it was diffused by the wholesale emigration of Greeks into the oriental lands of Alexander's conquests. In the eighteenth century, when Winckelmann and others were discovering the 'purity' of classical Greek art (and Greek culture in general), scholars and dilettantes alike, scorning the 'decadent' Greek world after Alexander as unworthy of being called Hellenic, seized upon the epithet Hellen*istic*—Greek*ish*, rather than Greek—to designate the culture of the last three centuries BC in the eastern Mediterranean, the centuries between Alexander and the complete envelopment of the area by the expanding might of Rome. In this vein, the *Oxford English Dictionary*, for example, a product of the late nineteenth century, defines Hellenistic in part as 'a. Applied to the modified form of the Greek language, with many foreign elements, current in Egypt, Syria and other countries after the time of Alexander the Great. b. Of or pertaining to the ancient Greeks of this later age, when the true Hellenic characteristics were modified by foreign elements'.

Contrasting sharply with those disdainful attitudes, though as yet without significant impact on our undergraduate teaching, twentieth-century scholarship has devoted increasing attention to the Hellenistic world, which is now seen as a vital link in the history of Western civilization. An early signal of that changing attitude was the lecture delivered in Oxford by M. Rostovtzeff soon after the First World War. It began:

Many years of close study of the history of the ancient world have convinced me that one of the most important epochs in the evolution of the world is the Hellenistic period, *i.e.* the three centuries after Alexander the Great. I am sure that, if we desire to understand the peculiarities of Greek genius and the subsequent history of civilization, this epoch is quite as important as the flourishing period of Greek politics and the time of the Roman world empire. . . . Athens moulded everlasting specimens of beauty and thought. The Greeks of the Hellenistic period, continuing the work of the Athenians, made these specimens accessible to millions. They have handed them down to us and made it possible for us to establish on them, as a base, the foundations first of European, and now of our world culture.[1]

No Greek city of any consequence emerged unscathed from the ravages of the Peloponnesian War of 431–404 BC, history's first demonstration of the universal disaster wrought by a world war. The ensuing decades of the early fourth century BC saw thousands of farmers unable or unwilling to return to the devastated land. Without visible means of support, they crowded into the cities, living from hand to mouth. The only employment open to large numbers of men was to sign on as mercenary soldiers in the pay of a foreign prince or power. The best-known instance of that activity, the expedition of The Ten Thousand whose story Xenophon tells in his *Anabasis*, included men from every part of the Greek world, not omitting even Sparta, which had won the Peloponnesian War and was supposedly luxuriating in the spoils of its victory. In the mercenaries' home cities, meanwhile, the pressing economic problems remained unresolved, and revolutionary cries for redistribution of land and cancellation of debts began to be heard. Some alarmed 'haves' began to advocate a policy of mass emigration, of opening up foreign lands, as a solution to the discontent of their 'have-nots'. A clarion call for such a programme came from the orator Isokrates. As early as *c.*380 BC—just about the time when Plato was composing his *Republic*, his prescription for an ideal state—Isokrates tried to rouse the Greek cities to unite in an invasion of the Persian Empire, an action which he justified on several grounds. First, it would end the Persian king's intrusions into Greek affairs. Next, in his words, 'it is far nobler to war with him for his kingdom than to dispute amongst ourselves over hegemony'. And lastly, by seizing just the nearest areas of the Persian Empire, the Greek cities would have enough land to distribute to their 'many who lack the daily necessities'. That plea fell on deaf ears, and Isokrates despaired of the Greek cities, but not of his idea. Years later, seeing the possibility of a new champion, he addressed the same plea to King Philip of Macedon, urging him to place himself at the head of such a crusade. That, but with no such altruistic motive, was in fact the direction in which Philip was heading. His first concern was to dominate the Greek cities to his south and east. That done, and his army thus protected against sabotage from behind, he began to plan the invasion of Persia. He was assassinated, but his son Alexander, who succeeded to the throne at the age of eighteen, lost little time in launching the attack.[2]

Alexander's conquest of the Persian Empire did, in fact, open up vast areas for Greek settlement, especially in Syria and Egypt. The young king's sudden death, however, was followed by a twenty-year period of uncertainty, during which his generals fought out the issue of the succession. By the end of the fourth century the situation had stabilized—Ptolemy ruled in Egypt, Seleukos in Syria, Antigonos in Macedon—and the rush of immigrants began. There was enough land in the 'New World' of the eastern Mediterranean for all the Greeks who wanted it. In addition, there were unprecedented business opportunities for the shrewd go-getter, government careers with rapid advancement for the well-connected and the competent, and royal patronage beckoning the practitioners of the arts and sciences to the new world capital, Alexandria.

Alexandria was founded in 331 BC. In 30 BC Octavian annexed Egypt, the last of the Hellenistic kingdoms to undergo Roman conquest and annexation. Those intervening 300 years have (as already noted in the opening paragraph) long been regarded as a time when the descendants of the Greeks who settled in the lands of the Near East ceased to be Greeks and became instead Graeco-Syrians, Graeco-Egyptians, and other such amalgams.[3] That concept gained wide currency on the authority of Johann Gustav Droysen's *Geschichte des Hellenismus*, the first volume of which appeared in 1836, the year before the young Victoria ascended the British throne. In those days (and long after) the spirit of the recently deceased G. W. F. Hegel dominated the philosophy of history, and the Hegelian trinity of thesis–antithesis–synthesis, as applied by Droysen to the Hellenistic world, produced the formula: Greek + Oriental = fusion of the two. It is only in the last half-century that a series of careful analytical studies, based on an accumulation of documentary evidence not previously available, has revealed the fallacy of the fusion hypothesis as a basis for understanding the history of Hellenistic times.[4]

Where people of two cultures, speaking different languages, live in close proximity, something of each is bound to rub off on the other. But what has now become clear, and becomes clearer with each new study, is that in Hellenistic Egypt such mutual influences were minimal.[5] From top to bottom, as we now see, the dominant socio-political characteristic of the country was not coalescence, but rather the coexistence of two discrete entities: 'we' and 'they', the conquerors and the conquered. The king himself had two distinct aspects reflecting the cleavage: in one he was the incarnation of an ideal of kingship formulated by Greek philosophers (as, for example, in Aristotle's *Politics*), while in the other, he retained for the Egyptians the role of successor and continuator of their line of Pharaohs. That duality, or dichotomy, mirrored the situation in the country as a whole, with its small privileged class of Macedonian and Greek origin, and its large mass of the native population, subjected and exploited, helpless victims of repeated abuses perpetrated not only by private individuals in the lordly immigrant class, but also—despite an officially proclaimed benevolent despotism—by office-holders in the royal administration.[6]

To American ears these words almost inevitably recall the conditions which prevailed in large parts of the South after the Civil War: a light-skinned minority ruling over nominally free but effectively subjugated dark-skinned masses. There is, however, one fundamental difference in the comparison: the Ptolemies' policy was not racially motivated. On the contrary, as we shall see in this book, small numbers of 'Hellenizing' native Egyptians were accorded admission to the privileged class to fulfil the needs of the civil and military services—needs which increased as time went on. Even so, the recent riots in the Black ghettoes of American cities or South African townships had their parallels in Ptolemaic Egypt, where we can count ten native revolts between 245 and 50 BC. There may, of course, have been others which do not appear in the surviving sources. And a recently published papyrus, in the collection of the University of Michigan, reveals that a royal proclamation issued on the day corresponding in our reckoning to 12 November 198 BC legalized the enslavement of Egyptians seized as booty by any of the king's soldiers in the course of 'the rebellion in the up-country'.[7]

The conditions of life in Ptolemaic Egypt are now known to us in intimate (if uneven) detail from a unique source: the thousands of Greek and hundreds of Demotic (i.e. Egyptian) papyri of Hellenistic date that have been found in Egypt in the past hundred years. While small numbers of papyri have been found in a few locations outside Egypt, no other part of the ancient world has provided us with such source material in such abundance. Unearthed by clandestine diggers as well as by officially sanctioned archaeologists, the papyri are now to be found in collections all over Europe and the United States as well as in Egypt itself—in museums, libraries, universities, and in private hands. Except that they have been darkened and dessicated (and consequently often fragmented) by their centuries of interment in the dry sands which preserved them from rotting away, the papyri present themselves to us today exactly as they were when written upon in antiquity. They include manuscripts of great (and not so great) works of literature previously lost to the modern world, and, in even greater numbers, documents of all kinds, on subjects from the gravest of public affairs to the most trivial of private concerns—in short, anything and everything that we also customarily commit to paper. Displaying to us their authentic, original texts—in contrast to the literary artistry and interpretative selectivity of the historical works surviving from antiquity—the papyri bring us into direct contact with the lives of the Greeks who settled in Egypt, and of the Egyptians among whom they settled.

The reader will observe, and no doubt wonder at, the absence from this book of a chapter on Alexandria, the Ptolemies' capital city, the commercial and cultural centre of the post-classical Greek world. The reason for the omission lies in the nature of the extant sources. As a result of constant inhabitation down through the centuries, Alexandria has left scant archaeological remains of its ancient greatness. Alexandrian papyri, too, are practically non-existent, having decayed in the damp soil of the Nile Delta. (Papyri found elsewhere do, of course, sometimes relate to Alexandria; and one Delta location has yielded a few lots of papyri preserved in a carbonized state, but these date from the time of Roman rule, after the Ptolemies.) Thus our evidence on Alexandria remains, for the most part, embedded in ancient literature known to the modern world since the Renaissance, and that literature, in contrast to the recent finds that constitute the fundament of this book, does not provide the kind of illumination that the papyri (and some inscriptions) shed on the life of the Greeks in the settlements up-river from Alexandria. As recently expressed by a noted French legal scholar,

What interests us here is to seize, in their essential elements, the conditions and the modalities of the persistence of Hellenism in the individuals whom Alexander's conquests and his successors' incentives drew to the conquered 'barbarian' lands, where they appear to us [in the papyri] as military and administrative officers, and as the economic beneficiaries of the Macedonian domination. How did one stay a Greek when a military reservist settled in a country village? . . . How did the Ptolemaic monarchy resolve the difficult problems presented by the prolonged presence of Greek-speaking immigrants in the non-Greek village areas, where the maintenance of a Greek identity was regarded by the regime as a vital [socio-]political imperative?[8]

Some of the answers to these questions are found in this book. The evidence that has accumulated in the past hundred years includes several groups of documents which, though the individual papyri are now usually scattered among various collections in different parts of the world, are revealed by their contents to have belonged to, or concerned, a single individual or family. The special historical value of such archives is self-evident. The record-keeping practices of modern societies leave students of modern history with an embarrassment of such riches, which they have come to expect as a matter of course. In contrast, for the historian of antiquity, who must

work with such monuments and records as have survived the
centuries, the discovery of an archive, large or small, is a
special event. A notable example is the wall at Apollo's
famous shrine in Delphi, which, when excavated a hundred
years ago, was discovered to be inscribed with hundreds of
slave manumissions carried out under the protection of the
god. The biggest find to date of papyri was made just before
the First World War by peasants digging for compost in the
ruins of the ancient village of Philadelphia, on the desert's
edge not far from Cairo. There they came upon close to 2,000
papyri comprising the files of a man named Zēnōn, who in the
mid-third century BC managed a vast estate, operated almost
like a medieval manor, on land that Ptolemy II had bestowed
(as a revocable—and, in fact, later revoked—gift) upon his
finance minister, one Apollonios. Those outstanding finds
have, understandably, evoked extensive scholarly literature.
The chapters of this book are devoted to smaller and less well-
known archives. While these sources have not lacked for
commentators among specialists in papyrology, the pages that
follow aim to make their contents and lessons available to a
wider public, with each chapter illuminating some aspect or
element of society in the three centuries of Ptolemaic rule in
Egypt.

I

The Backdrop: Eldorado on the Nile

Long before the Hellenistic age, Egypt had become fixed in
the Greek consciousness as a land of exotic mystery and
fabulous wealth. That stereotype appears in Greek literature
of all genres and periods, from the Homeric epics on. The
Iliad, the composition of which, in its present form, most
scholars now place in the eighth century BC, contains a single
mention of Egypt. The verse, the 382nd of Book 9, used
sometimes to be rejected by scholars as an interpolation of a
later age, but modern editors are now generally satisfied that
it is genuine, and, together with confirmatory archaeological
finds, it gives evidence of pre-existing contact between the
Greek world and Egypt. In the *Odyssey*, later by half a century
or so, the name of Egypt appears almost two dozen times. In
four of these instances the wealth and fertility of the land are
emphasized, and in two other places the poet tells of
unsuccessful pirate raids against Egypt's Mediterranean
coast. These last episodes are dim reminiscences of events that
occurred in the thirteenth and twelfth centuries BC, when the
eastern Mediterranean was swept by mass migrations, in the
course of which some groups, called 'Peoples of the Sea' on the
triumphal monuments of the Pharaohs Merneptah and
Ramses III, attempted to invade Egypt and were driven off.[1]
Significant, too, in the *Odyssey* are geographical details that
can only have come from eyewitness accounts, notably the
references to the river Nile and to the offshore islet of Pharos,
later the site of the famous lighthouse. In the hundred years
after the composition of the *Odyssey*, Greek mercenaries and
merchants became active in Egypt, and before the end of the
seventh century their numbers had increased to the point
where they were permitted to organize their fortified trading
centre at Naukratis, in the Nile Delta, as a locally autonomous
Greek city. In the same period another sizeable concentration
of Greeks was established at Memphis, which Greek mercen-

aries helped the Pharaoh Psammetichus I (664–610 BC) recapture from a rival claimant to the throne.

Before Alexander the Great, the most famous Greek visitor to Egypt was the fifth-century historian Herodotus, whose account of the strange people and customs of the land of the Nile fills the second book of his *Histories*. Egypt was known to the Greeks of those days as a land where a tourist or a trader might visit, where—as we have just seen—a man might go to find employment (military, at the very least) or even to take up permanent residence as a trade representative or entrepreneur. But those Greeks numbered only some thousands at most, and even in prosperity they never ceased to be aware that they were living in a foreign land at the pleasure of its ruler. Alexander's conquests changed all that, making Egypt a part of the Greek 'New World', a land of opportunity for all—all Greeks that is, and also a relatively small number of natives who could aspire to government careers under the new regime (the first requirement being to have gained some competence in the Greek language).

A major accomplishment of Alexander's brief stay in Egypt, one destined to have lasting significance in the history of the Western world, was his foundation of a new capital for the country, a city bearing his name, Alexandria. By situating it on the Mediterranean coast he emphasized that it was a part of the Greek world: indeed, its official designation, which it retained for centuries thereafter, was Alexandria-by-Egypt (rather than in or of Egypt). And in thus locating the capital city in the Nile Delta, he also established a Greek counterweight to rival Memphis and to dim the lustre and nationalistic appeal of that religious and political centre which had been for millennia the Pharaohs' capital in Lower (i.e. northern) Egypt. Soon after becoming king, Ptolemy I followed Alexander's example and attracted settlers to another Greek city, Ptolemais, which he founded not far from Thebes, the indigenous capital of Upper Egypt. From Alexandria and the Mediterranean to Egypt's southern frontier just beyond Elephantinē and the First Cataract of the Nile, smaller settlements of Greek-speaking immigrants and their descendants dotted the landscape under the Ptolemaic dynasty, tiny enclaves of Hellenism proudly disdaining the 'barbarian' masses by whom they were surrounded. But, as we shall see both in this and in later chapters, proximity and daily contact led inevitably to some breaches in the exclusionary barriers. Later generations of Greeks, born in Egypt, were less hostile to intermarriage with Egyptians than their immigrant ancestors had been, especially in the southernmost settlements, where the Greeks were fewest in numbers and farthest removed from the Hellenizing aura of Alexandria.

Getting There

From near and far they flocked to the land of opportunity. We have records of immigrants from as far east as Sinope, a city in the remotest recess of the Black Sea, as far north as Illyria, Macedon, and Thrace, as far west as Syracuse in Sicily and possibly even Marseilles (which was founded as a Greek colony *c.*600 BC). In one recorded instance, a party of 'recruiting sergeants' sent out by the first or second Ptolemy succeeded in enrolling mercenaries originating in Boiotia, Thessaly, Magnesia in Asia Minor, Crete, and Malta. In all, the thousands of individuals we encounter in the papyri of Ptolemaic date came from more than 200 different places in the Greek world.

The *Mimes* of the Hellenistic poet Herondas are a series of vignettes, some of them slightly bawdy, of everyday life. In the first of the series, composed in or about 270 BC, a young woman sits at home in a Greek city, brooding over the long absence of her 'man' (whether husband or lover is left vague). A procuress comes to press the case for a liaison with a customer of hers:

It's ten months since Mandris went off to Egypt, and you haven't heard a single word from him. He's drunk from a new cup of love, and he's forgotten you. Aphrodité's headquarters are down there. In Egypt they have everything that exists or is made anywhere in the wide world: wealth, sports, power, excellent climate, fame, sights, philosophers, gold, young men, a shrine of the sibling gods, an enlightened king, the Museum, wine—in short, every good thing he might desire. And women! more women, by Hades' Persephoné, than the sky boasts stars. And looks! like the goddesses who once incited Paris to judge their beauty.[2]

The lure of the Ptolemaic Eldorado is reflected also in the life and works of the poet Theokritos. A native of Syracuse, he left his intolerably provincial home town to seek fame and fortune in a more congenial cultural atmosphere, and after some wanderings he found them in Alexandria, where he settled *c.*270 BC. The fourteenth of his thirty-one *Idylls* depicts a young man, Aischinēs, fuming because his mistress has gone off with a rival. He is thinking of taking a sea voyage to forget—or, as he says, 'to unlove'—her. A friend offers the following counsel:

If you really mean to emigrate, Ptolemy is the freeman's paymaster, the best there is. What sort of man is he otherwise? The best there is—considerate, a man of wit and taste, partial to the ladies, the height of courtesy, knows who his friends are (and even better, who are not), bestower of much upon many, no denier of favours, as befits a king. . . . Well, if you are ready to clasp the military cloak on your right shoulder, if you have the courage to plant your legs firmly to withstand the attack of a bold warrior, get you quickly to Egypt.[3]

Mandris and Aischines were but two of the thousands of men, young and not so young, who joined the 'goldrush' to Ptolemaic Egypt. No doubt many were as faithless as Mandris appears to have been when they got there, but no doubt many others took their wives and children along, or sent for them after they were settled.

Soon after becoming king, the first Ptolemy began to improve the double harbour at Alexandria with a view to making his capital the leading commercial centre of the Mediterranean world. As one of his measures toward that end he engaged the architect Sostratos of Knidos to design and direct the construction of a lighthouse which would make the port approachable even by night. The structure, in three superimposed 'setbacks', was erected upon—and ever after called by the name of—the islet Pharos, which lay conveniently in front of the harbour entrances. The lighthouse came into service in 280 BC, early in the reign of Ptolemy II, and was soon hailed as one of the Seven Wonders of the World. It rose, we are told in what is probably an exaggeration, 400 cubits (210 metres) into the sky, and was equipped with pulleyed lifts as well as stairs. It is reported that the flames from the fire lit on its top could be seen at night from more than fifty kilometres away, intensified by reflecting mirrors. An inscribed plaque dedicated the lighthouse 'to the saviour gods, for the protection of those at sea'. The saviour gods of Greek seafarers were Castor and Pollux, the Dioskouroi, but in this context the expression undoubtedly has a *double entendre*, embracing the ruling king and queen as a second pair of divine protectors. The Pharos served shipping for over a thousand years; it was damaged by heavy seas in the sixth century, and was finally crumbled by earthquakes in the fourteenth.[4]

Was it an easy trip to Egypt from the Aegean and other parts of the Mediterranean world? The brief answer to that question is yes and no. The land and sea routes, especially those from Asia Minor and the Aegean islands, had been in use for centuries. But antiquity never developed anything resembling a regular passenger service. To take ship you went down to the waterfront and enquired around until you found a cargo vessel headed (if you were lucky) for your destination. Failing that, you would have to settle for one departing in the general direction in which you wanted to go. You then made your arrangement for passage with the skipper. In the summer time, with the Etesian winds blowing from the north, a direct run to Alexandria could be made in six days from the Piraeus, nine from Byzantion. But relatively few travellers had such good fortune. Most of the ships available were tramps, making stops to unload and then, like as not, waiting to find another cargo before setting sail again. The passengers, knowing they might have to change carriers *en route*, would often head for a major port, such as Ephesos, whence they could be sure of getting, without too long a wait, a coastal vessel for the rest of the journey. It must have taken many of the immigrants two weeks or more to reach Alexandria. An extant letter of 257 BC tells us how two travellers bound from Alexandria were blown off course to Lykia, where they hired a boat to take them along the coast to their proper destination in southern Asia Minor; that entire trip took two months, but the letter reporting the news took only nineteen days to get back to the village of Philadelphia in the Arsinoite nome, some 250 kilometres up-river from Alexandria.[5]

As there were on board the vessels of those days no cabins, lounges, or such amenities as we today take for granted, passengers had to provide for their own comfort and amusement. Occasional travellers, as well as immigrants, would take along not only clothing but also the household equipment needed for eating and sleeping—food, pots and pans, and bedding. For entertainment they had, first of all, the other passengers to talk to. Gambling must have helped both players and onlookers to while away some of the time. In good weather there was the perennial fascination of looking up at the clouds in the sky and at the water scudding by. In sailing vessels there is also the attraction of watching the crew work the ship. And those who were literate would doubtless bring along some reading matter.

The amusements were possible so long as the weather held fine. But sudden onslaughts of wind and wave often make travel in and around the Aegean hazardous, especially in the winter and early spring. Even the biggest freighters could then be blown off course, and on smaller craft the issue would often be not holding course but simply staying alive by riding out the storm. The letter of 257 BC cited above has shown us one party of travellers buffeted about and delayed by the elements. Another, doubtless the most familiar such case, is that of St Paul on his journey to Rome. He was on a good-sized ship, with 276 passengers on board. When the gale struck, passengers pitched in to help the crew jettison the tackle. Later, as their situation grew more perilous, they helped to dump the cargo of grain overboard. 'The alternative to keeping afloat was death, since ancient vessels carried no lifeboats; the ship's boat, which might accommodate a dozen people at best, was for harbour service [as a tug] not saving lives'. Instances are reported where crews of foundering ships tried to escape in the skiff, leaving the passengers to sink or swim. Then again, even if kept afloat, the vessel might be driven ashore by the storm and wrecked. 'The ship was rushing along', one ancient account narrates, 'under full canvas because we couldn't shorten sail. Time and again we laid hands on the lines but gave up because they were jammed in the blocks. And secretly we began to be equally afraid that, even if we escaped from the raging sea, we could be approaching land in the dead of night in this helpless condition'.[6]

The list of major perils that the voyager might encounter on the high seas is not yet complete. There was also the danger that pirates might swoop down and seize the ship, killing any on board who offered resistance and hauling off the rest to be sold as slaves. In the third century BC, when the powerful fleets of Egypt and of the mercantile island of Rhodes patrolled the shipping lanes, the incidence of piracy was sharply curtailed, but the freebooters were never completely driven from the sea. And so, what with delays, storms, shipwrecks, enslavement, and even death to contemplate as possible concomitants or results of a sea voyage, it is small wonder that many, particularly immigrants coming from Syria and Asia Minor, often preferred to make their way to Egypt along the coastal road—the Via Maris, as the Romans later called it—even though overland travel was slower and costlier than sailing. As we shall observe presently, along with the multitudes of Greeks there were fair numbers of Jews who also immigrated into Egypt in the third and second centuries BC; for them of course, the coastal road was the handiest route connecting Judaea with Egypt.

Living There

THE FIRST AND SECOND GENERATIONS

If there was an 'immigration and naturalization' service through which the new arrivals had to pass on reaching Egypt, there is no hint of it in the sources. There were, we do know, numerous customs dues. Travellers accompanied by slaves had to pay an import tax before they were allowed to take them in. Goods of many kinds were subject to *ad valorem* duties that could run as high as 50 per cent, but that was in the ordinary course of business; there is no suggestion that the immigrants' personal or household effects would be classed as dutiable. As for the immigrants themselves, we have no information at all pointing to any restrictions or exclusions: it would appear that an 'open door' policy prevailed, welcoming all who chose to come. Departure from Egypt, however, required an exit permit.

'The foreigners who arrive by sea,' remarks the writer of a letter of 258 BC, 'the merchants, the forwarding agents and others, bring with them their own local currencies'. Some traders came bringing luxury imports (such as slaves and horses) for the court and the *nouveaux riches*. Many more came for various of Egypt's famous export commodities, most notably grain and papyrus rolls, the writing paper of antiquity. Before they could enter the country and move about freely they would have to exchange the money they brought with them for the king's coinage, which circulated only in Egypt and was the only legal tender there. The banks charged a commission (perhaps as high as 10 per cent) on the exchange, and they were obligated to forward the foreign specie to the royal treasury to be melted down and reissued as Ptolemaic coinage.[7]

The Civilians

As far as we can tell, the Ptolemaic government left those who came in search of the widely reported get-rich-quick opportunities more or less to find their own way. In addition to the centuries-old Greek city of Naukratis and the more recently founded cities of Alexandria and Ptolemais, sizeable settlements of Greek traders quickly expanded in several Egyptian population centres, such as Memphis and some of the other capitals of the three dozen or so nomes (districts) into which Egypt was divided for administrative purposes. The newcomers would naturally tend to gravitate, on arrival, to one or another of the Greek-speaking communities, where they could feel more quickly at home in a strange land. Many of them, moreover, had been preceded by relatives or friends, or friends of friends, by whom they might expect to be received and assisted, sometimes with money, more often with words and letters of recommendation. Such a letter, especially if addressed by someone of consequence to a high official or other powerful figure, could do wonders in opening doors to lucrative opportunities in business or government service. Many such letters have been found among the papyri. Here is one written in Alexandria *c.*250 BC to the manager of the finance minister's huge estate at Philadelphia, in the Arsinoite nome.

Asklepiadēs to Zēnōn, greeting. Philōn, who will hand you this letter, has been known to me for some time. He is sailing up [the Nile] with a view to being employed in one or another department under Philiskos [an official in the nome]. Please, then, get to know him, and introduce him to other persons of standing; assist him actively both for my sake and for that of the young man himself—he is deserving of your special consideration, as will be evident to you too if you receive him into your hands. Goodbye.[8]

Philon, the bearer of that letter, had obviously come to Egypt with an eye to personal advancement. Employment in government service, from the middle to the highest ranks (the lowest being generally left to natives who could communicate in Greek), was one of the major areas of opportunity open to the incoming Greeks. The administrative system developed under the Ptolemies was one of 'checks and double checks', which of necessity called into being an extensive bureaucratic apparatus staffed by an army of functionaries. We shall be observing elements of that bureaucracy in action all through this book.

Another type of immigrant from Greek lands was the man of some wealth—great or modest, as the case might be—who came to Egypt in search of good investments, preferably those yielding quick profits. Some became shopkeepers, like the three wine merchants of the village of Kerkesoucha who, in 218 BC, filed a complaint against an Egyptian farmer who took their money but delivered, so they said, less than the quantity contracted for. Men with greater resources found opportunities all about them, in industry, banking, import and export, shipping, and above all in moneylending and tax farming. The Ptolemaic state, to be sure, retained seigneurial rights over a considerable number of economic activities, among the most important being the production and distribution of vegetable oils (the 'butter' and lubricants of antiquity), the import and/or export of certain commodities, and the operation of banks. But generally the government would let to the highest bidder the exclusive right to engage in a particular activity in a given area for a given period of time—in short, an entrepreneur's dream. Individually or by pooling resources, men with liquid assets engaged in spirited competition for those lucrative contracts.[9]

Moneylending was a particularly brisk business. Bottomry loans (made to shipowners for voyages, on the security of the vessel) appear to have been especially profitable, but the extant evidence on these is as scanty as the evidence for ordinary personal loans is abundant. Short-term loans were made to private parties for all sorts of purposes and needs, and on all sorts of security, not excluding the person of the debtor. Interest on such loans in the rest of the Hellenistic world was mostly in the range of 8–10 per cent per annum, but the Ptolemies, by royal edict, allowed a maximum of 2 per cent a month, or 24 per cent a year. At that rate a man could look to double his capital in four years, five at most. The likeliest explanation of the striking differential in the interest rates is that in remote, self-sufficient Egypt, where the agricultural villages persisted to a great extent in the practices of their traditional barter economy, coined money was and remained scarce in comparison with the rest of the Greek world, where a monetary economy had prevailed for centuries. The situation peculiar to Egypt probably also explains why the Ptolemies chose to create a unique internal coinage of their own, distinct from and not immiscible with any of the coinages that circulated in the rest of the Hellenistic world: in that way, while the relatively poor Aegean world would never be the source of immense infusions of capital, whatever money did come into Egypt would stay there, increasing the supply available within the country. Even so, however, the supply rarely kept up with the demand, and the shortfall was aggravated by the financial drain of the repeated wars with Seleucid Syria. One result was that by the beginning of the second century BC, silver coinage had practically disappeared from the internal economy of Ptolemaic Egypt, to be replaced by copper in a silver–copper ratio of about 500 : 1.

No doubt to compensate for or attenuate somewhat the high interest allowed, another Ptolemaic law (said by tradition to have been the continuation or revival of one instituted by a Pharaoh of the eighth century BC) provided that the total amount of interest collected on a loan might not exceed the principal. But extant documents reveal that in rates of interest charged, the legal maximum was often exceeded with impunity, and it therefore seems safe to suppose that the limitation on the total amount of interest was also circumvented rather easily. In short, there was money, often big money, to be made in moneylending.

Shipping was another activity that attracted investors. As the need for bottomry loans was constant, profits were practically guaranteed. The basic commodity requiring transportation by water was the portion of the harvests that the government collected as taxes. In vessels large and small—with, on present evidence, capacities of 200 to 10,000 artabs, or 5 to 250 tons—those cargoes were moved from the country districts to Alexandria, whence much of the grain was exported abroad. As the fleet of state-owned barges was (by design, apparently) not very large, there was a need, especially at peak periods, for supplementary carriers. The attractiveness of the enterprise to the private investor is eloquently attested by the fact that among the identifiable shipowners we find men and women in the upper crust of Ptolemaic society, including the court itself; one of the queens, Kleopatra II or III, owned some boats in her own name. It goes without saying that these people were only owners, who did not involve themselves in the actual operation of the vessels; for that they hired a skipper for each boat, and left him to handle the necessary details.[10]

Tax farming, a common institution in the Greek homeland, was yet another means to quick and easy profits, the more so as in Ptolemaic Egypt it merely required putting up the money and standing by to check the books and bank accounts of the local officials, the king's agents, who did the actual tax collecting. In other words, the Ptolemaic tax farmer functioned as a guarantor of a specified amount of tax revenue, not as a collector of taxes. Every year the principal taxes of a prescribed area were auctioned off, each separately, to the highest bidder, from whom the state then received the proferred sum in advance—in one lump sum or, more often, in instalments. The purchaser of the contract, or tax farmer, would expect to recoup his outlay, with profit, from the actual receipts deposited by the state collectors in the local bank. A papyrus roll in the Louvre, from which the extract in the next paragraph is quoted, shows how carefully every detail of the procedure was spelled out. Particularly noteworthy is the specification that the purchaser of the contract would have to make good any deficits. Such shortfalls doubtless occurred from time to time, the result of crop failure or other aleatory causes. But the risk to the tax farmer appears, overall, to have been slight. Neither it, nor the quantities of 'red tape' revealed by the regulations, appear to have constituted real deterrents to spirited bidding for most of the contracts.

The Louvre document dates from the year 203/2 BC. It begins with the royal 'we'.

We offer for sale [to the highest bidder] the tax-farming contracts in the Oxyrhynchite nome for . . . the [coming] year 2 for twelve months and five intercalary days. You are to purchase the contracts in the lawful manner, and let no one have cause to denounce or decry but in the best possible manner conduct your affairs according to the laws, ordinances, edicts, and amendments promulgated by us for each tax-farming contract. In carrying out the contracts make no deduction on any pretence whatsoever from the sum due the Treasury, and engage in no defalcation, being assured that any shortfalls will be collected from you.

Those who obtain the contracts shall present to the [nome's] finance officer and royal secretary sureties for the full amount of the contract plus 10 per cent . . . within thirty days from the sale . . . . Within x days of their recept the liability declarations of the sureties shall be deposited and indexed in the royal banks, bearing the seals of the said officials and of the banker. The latter will enter in his monthly records, clearly written, the details of the liability declarations—the value of the property placed under lien, who the guarantors are, and which properties each has placed under lien for the guarantee; also the certification of the officials that they have verified that the pledges they have accepted are worth the [stated] sums. . . .

If any of those holding a contract fail to provide sureties within the statutory time, their contracts shall be resold, and if a lower bid results, the difference shall be collected from them forthwith. . . . Those obtaining the contracts may subcontract, apprising the finance officer and royal secretary, and the subcontractors shall present sureties to the aforesaid [officials], which sureties shall not be counted toward those to be presented by the tax farmers [i.e. the prime contractors]. The liability declarations of these sureties are to be processed in the same way. . . .

The accounts of the contract shall be settled with the tax farmers monthly from the amounts paid into the bank [by the collectors]. . . . For the payments they shall obtain from the banker receipts signed by witnesses. If they do not follow this procedure, they will have no claim to the payments. If any of the tax farmers have obtained several contracts and make a profit on some and fall short on others, the profits shall be calculated against the deficits [i.e. to reduce or cancel them out]. . . . No one shall join in partnership with those obtaining the contracts except those whose names were recorded at the time of the sale. If any persons act in violation of this [order], the one taking on a partner shall pay a fine of twenty talents, and the one becoming a partner twenty talents. If any [tax farmers in partnership] owe money on their contracts, collection shall be made from any one or from all of them.[11]

A very recent piece of research has revealed yet another money-making opportunity that offered quick profits. Later in this chapter we shall examine the privileges accorded those immigrants who were given allotments of land in partial compensation for enrolment in the military reserve. Many, probably most, of those military settlers never had any intention of working the land themselves (and some who tried soon gave up), but looked forward instead to leasing their allotments to native farmers while they enjoyed the existence of *rentiers* in some Greek setting, urban or quasi-urban. Individuals with ready cash were quick to step in as middlemen. They would contract to lease entire allotments from their holders, usually paying or lending them cash in advance, with a portion of the crop to follow after the harvest to provide the allotment holders with the staff of life. Then the middlemen would sublease, in plots large and small, at substantially higher rents, to landless Egyptian peasants, who would perform the actual cultivation.[12]

After this array of glittering prizes, it is important to add that not every Greek immigrant to Ptolemaic Egypt became a millionaire overnight. For many the new Eldorado on the Nile turned out to be a land of false promise and deluded hopes. These 'failures' never rose out of the ranks of the poor, eking out their existences in the same menial, lowly occupations as the Egyptians. Later in this chapter, for example, we shall encounter a Greek muleteer, who took an Egyptian as wife.

The Military

In contrast to the immigrants who entered the business world, going essentially their own way, those who came to Ptolemaic Egypt for employment in the armed forces, whether as mercenaries hired for a stated term or as permanent settlers constituting an active reserve, were 'processed' by agents and officers of the crown from the moment they set foot on Egyptian soil. As a result, the papyri and inscriptions from Ptolemaic Egypt are replete with information—sporadic, to be sure—about the lives led by those immigrants and their descendants.

In historical perspective, the military system of the Ptolemies evokes a strong sense of *déjà vu*. Ptolemy I probably, and Ptolemy II certainly, began to find mercenaries an unsatisfactory basis for a reliable military establishment. As the mercenaries signed on for finite, relatively short periods, it was never certain how many of them would elect to renew their contracts. Further, they were a drain on the Treasury, as they had to be paid in specie; in fact, they sometimes insisted on being paid in a coinage with which they were familiar, as we deduce from a find of silver tetradrachms which are Athenian in type but were minted in Egypt.[13] Although no Hellenistic ruler ever felt able to dispense entirely with the use of mercenaries, Ptolemy II and his successors, in a throwback to a system created long before by the Pharaohs, pursued increasingly a policy of fostering a permanent, hereditary military class, which, settled upon the land in times of peace, could be quickly mobilized in emergencies. It is worth noting, too, that while the vast majority of the military settlers were of Greek and Macedonian origin, other non-Egyptians, for example Idoumaians (Edomites) from south of the Dead Sea, were also accepted, and Jews too were encouraged to enrol, especially after 167 BC when the Maccabean revolt liberated Judaea from the rule of Seleucid Syria, the Ptolemies' principal rival for hegemony in the region.[14]

Billets   Of the recruits arriving from abroad some few were retained in Alexandria, to bolster the palace guard and other élite corps. The great majority, mercenaries and settlers alike, were dispatched to different places in the up-country, where they were billeted upon the local population, either permanently or until separate domiciles could be built for them.

Throughout history, the billeting of soldiers in private homes has been a cause of friction between civilians and military. Even when the billets are paid for, there is helpless resentment on the part of the reluctant hosts, and the arrogant soldiers often add insult to injury by behaving as if they own the place. And when the billets are requisitioned, as was the case in Ptolemaic Egypt, the effect is, additionally, that of a continuing tax imposed upon hapless victims.

Among the earliest Ptolemaic documents in existence, dating from 276 to 261 BC, are half a dozen royal edicts decrying a variety of abuses perpetrated by billeted soldiery. One edict forbids a soldier who has a billet to claim another, on pain of losing both. A second edict orders that a soldier is to occupy half, and no more, of the structure in which he is housed, leaving half to the owner; here the penalty for violation was a heavy fine.[15]

Sometimes the soldiers even quarrelled amongst themselves and resorted to violence over preferred billets, as we see in the following letter, whose date corresponds to 10 August 259 BC.

To King Ptolemy greeting from Areus, rower serving on the corvette [under the command] of Polemon. I am wronged by Kephalon. After I was assigned lodgings by Moschion, Kephalon—although there was no quarrel between him and me—forced his way into my billet, threw my furnishings out into the street, and beat me in an attempt to force me out too. But as I refused to budge and called the neighbours to witness, and as a number of them ran up and rebuked him, he cleared off and I brought back my things that had been thrown out into the street. I therefore beg you, O king, to order the local police chief to look into the violence and the blows . . . [The rest is lost.]

Some five or ten years later the following letter was written to an otherwise unknown (to us) officer.

King Ptolemy to Antiochos, greeting. About the billeting of soldiers we hear that some instances of undue violence have occurred when, instead of waiting to be assigned lodgings by the finance officer [of the nome], they simply march into houses, eject the people and occupy the premises by force. Give orders, therefore, that this may not occur again: if they erect their own shelters, well and good, but if they need to be assigned billets the finance officers are to give them what is necessary. And when they give up their billets, they are to restore and release them, and are not to reserve them till they come back, as we hear they now do, renting them out to others or locking the rooms before they go off. . . .[16]

Despite the edicts and the orders, the abuses continued, for the impetus toward high-handedness was inherent in the situation itself, pitting as it did powerless 'hosts' against self-indulgent, armed 'guests'. Above we saw, from 259 BC, an incident where one soldier tried to force another out of his billet and move himself in; in Chapter 4 there is quoted from 221 BC the case of another who, assigned lodgings in a village, simply expelled the Egyptian owner of another house that he saw and liked better. Unable to offer direct resistance either to the billeting or to the abuses, house-owners discovered one ingenious subterfuge after another, only to find those in turn rendered unavailing, as we see in the following report sent in 242 BC to his superior by an officer in charge of billeting.

We find . . . that some houses assigned as billets have had their roofs pulled down by their owners, some of whom have also blocked up the doors of their houses or built altars up against them [so that they will appear to be sanctuaries]. This they have done with the aim of their not being billeted in. So please, as we are pinched for billets, give orders to compel owners of houses to remove the altars . . . so we can assign those houses to the works superintendents now arriving.[17]

Many a lodger, in order to ensure his family's privacy, went so far as to have a wall built dividing the house in half, and this quickly became a common, more or less accepted, practice. However, that too could be a source of dispute, as we see in the following complaint which was filed in 222 BC by a woman named Asia, a soldier's widow. Her name reveals her origin, and explains why she would have an altar of a Syrian deity in her house.

I am wronged by Pooris, the owner of my lodgings. My husband Machatas, being billeted in the village of Pelousion, divided the house with Pooris and built in his own half an altar to the Syrian goddess and Aphrodite Berenike [the reigning queen]. Between Pooris' half and my husband's there was a half-finished wall, and when I wanted to complete the wall so as to prevent crossing over into our quarters, Pooris stopped me from building, not that the wall is any of his business but making light of me because my husband is dead. I therefore beg you, O king, to instruct Diophanēs the strategos to write to Menandros the [village] police chief [to investigate and] if he finds the wall is ours, not to allow Poōris to prevent us from building it, and thus I, having fled to you for refuge, O king, will obtain justice. Farewell.[18]

Land Allotments In addition to their lodgings, the mercenaries received their pay, in cash. In contrast, each settler was given, instead of cash, a landholding in a subdivision carved out for the military reservists either from the king's own vast domain, or (by royal order) from the extensive temple lands, or from the large estates previously granted by the king to courtiers and other favourites. The parcel of land allotted to an individual was called in Greek *klēros*, the military settler *klērouchos* ('allotment holder'), 'cleruch' in its Anglicized form. Attracted by the very visible benefits of the cleruchs' privileged treatment, many a mercenary stayed on and had his status changed to that of military settler. But others preferred, while settling in as permanent residents, to retain their status of professional soldiers, a development that is particularly noticeable in the extant sources of the second century BC. As the ready supply of mercenaries from abroad showed signs of drying up at that time, the Ptolemaic regime, in a largely successful bid to retain their services, offered its professional soldiery a hereditary option essentially the same as that which the cleruchs enjoyed. We shall meet three families of such hereditary soldiery in Chapters 6 and 8.

As for the cleruchs, military rank played a major part in determining how big a parcel of land an individual would receive. The land measure was the *aroura*, the equivalent of 0.68 acres, or 0.275 hectares. The soldiers of the Pharaohs, according to Herodotus, had received allotments equal to twelve arouras each. Under the Ptolemies, members of the royal guard and of the cavalry were classified as holders of 50, 70, 80 or 100 arouras, the men of the infantry as holders of 20, 25, 30 or 40 arouras. For native Egyptians, who were admitted to cleruchic status after 217 BC (see p. 29), the range was only 5 to 30 arouras. In fact, however, the size of a *klēros* was often considerably smaller, sometimes somewhat larger, than the nominal classification figure. In many places, too, the administration used the cleruchic system as an instrument for increasing agricultural production: when assigned, many a *klēros* included, by design, a sizeable portion of uncultivated land, and it was expected that the prospect of profit would induce the cleruch to bring those marginal or waste areas into production. The government co-operated in that endeavour by undertaking an adjuvant programme of public works, especially in irrigation, as will appear in Chapter 2. As a further benefit, cleruchs paid lower taxes than others on the crops that their land produced.

Obviously, then, just as one billet was, or was deemed to be, better than another, so one *klēros* in a given area would be more desirable than another—the land would be better located, or of higher quality, and so forth. Although the very word *klēros* implied (at least originally) assignment by lottery, here too having friends in high places could be helpful in obtaining one of the better allotments, as we see in this letter of *c.*250 BC.

Asklepiades to Zenon, greeting. Erasis, who will hand you this letter, happens to be a relative and friend of mine. He brings with him his nephew Erilochos, a candidate for a land assignment. Please, then, take care of the gentlemen, see that they obtain a suitable billet—preferably in Philadelphia, so as to be near you, but at all events somewhere appropriate—and that in the land measurement they are not cheated. And if they have any other need of you, give them active assistance both for my sake and for that of the men themselves, for they are deserving of your special consideration. Goodbye.[19]

What portion of the land as a whole was given over to cleruchs? The answer to that question must have varied from locality to locality, as military and agricultural considerations dictated. Kerkeosiris, a village in the Arsinoite nome, is the only place for which we have comprehensive data, and then only for the year 118 BC. In that year the village's land area of some 4,700 arouras was categorized as follows:[20]

	% of total
royal land	52
cleruchic land	33

% of total

temple land	6
miscellaneous	9

The Greek Ambiance

'People change their skies, not their feelings, when they rush overseas', remarked the Roman poet Horace (*Epistles* 1.11.27). The Greek settlers lost little time in surrounding themselves as far as possible with the familiar scenery of life in their home cities. Immigrants generally do that, of course, as a way of helping themselves to feel at home in a strange land. The Greeks in Egypt had the further purpose of accentuating the social barriers that set them, the ruling élite, apart from the mass of natives all about them. Even the way their settlement was built could contribute toward their proud sense of Hellenism. In the north-east corner of the Arsinoite nome, for example, lay the village of Philadelphia, founded by Ptolemy II Philadelphos with the installation of some cleruchic units. A partial excavation of the ruins in the winter of 1908–9 revealed that the village was laid out on the rectangular 'grid' characteristic of Hellenistic cities. The streets, crossing at right angles divided the village into blocks measuring 100 × 200 Egyptian cubits (about 50 × 100 metres), each block containing twenty houses, separated here and there by narrow alleyways. Within the settlements like Philadelphia the principal Hellenic institutions—transplants, as it were, from the cities of Greece—were their temples and their gymnasia. Although the Greek gods began almost immediately to be syncretized, in varying degrees, with native deities of comparable attributes, the settlers continued to build their temples in the Greek colonnaded style, very different from the massive fortress-like Egyptian structures, and went on performing their worship along traditional Greek lines.

Even more fiercely than the temple, the gymnasium resisted invasion by Egyptians to the very end of the Ptolemaic era. A characteristic institution of Greek cities, the gymnasium was from very early times the centre for physical training and sports, a kind of exclusive club for the male citizenry, to which women and non-citizens were not admitted. From about the mid-fourth century BC it also served as the parade ground for military training of the ephebes, or citizen youth.

In Ptolemaic Egypt we find gymnasia not only in the Greek cities and the district capitals (some of them having more than one), but even in villages, even quite small ones, where Greek-speaking communities were established. Though the regime undoubtedly welcomed and even encouraged them as solidifiers of the privileged class upon whose support it depended, the gymnasia were not government institutions, or even state-subsidized. They were created to satisfy the aspirations of the people of Greek and Macedonian origin in their several localities, and the funding for construction and maintenance varied from place to place. Some, we know, were philanthropic gifts to the community from local benefactors, while for others the necessary funds were raised through contributions solicited from the interested families of soldiers, cleruchs, and civilians. Once built, the gymnasia trained the sons of those families and sponsored games to celebrate the festivals of the traditional gods and the royal cult; in short, they 'provided a common ground for soldier and citizen to share religious and educational traditions'.[21]

THE LATER GENERATIONS

Despite the xenophobic barriers erected by the Graeco-Macedonian communities, the circumstances of everyday intercourse led inevitably, with the passage of time, to some intermarriage with Egyptians. This was particularly true in the rural areas, beginning in the humbler strata of both populations, and gradually spreading among the military settlements, especially the more isolated detachments. It is a striking fact that in every intermarriage attested in extant documents it is a man of Greek or Macedonian origin who takes an Egyptian woman to wife. The reverse pairing—a Greek woman with an Egyptian man—may be supposed a priori to have occurred, but the fact that children acquired the legal status (Greek or Egyptian) of the father must have made intermarriages of that kind rare. In the earliest instance to which we can point, dating from 250 BC, the Greek husband is a lowly muleteer in a village in the Arsinoite nome, and the wife, whose name is not too clearly readable, appears to be an Egyptian. An intermarriage in which the husband may have been a military man is mentioned in a recently published papyrus of *c.*230 BC. Offspring of such mixed marriages bearing two names, one Greek, the other Egyptian, begin to appear in documents of the latter half of the third century, and the phenomenon becomes widespread thereafter.[22]

As the papyri of Ptolemaic date come from a number of places in the up-country, we are left with the impression of an almost mathematical progression: the farther a settlement was from an urban centre, most particularly from the Hellenizing influence of Alexandria, the more quickly and more readily it surrendered to the pressures of Egyptians eager to enter the class of privilege. In the more remote regions, the intermarriages had a two-way effect: Egyptian women thereby attained Greek status for their children and descendants, and the Greeks found it more and more comfortable, as time went on, to adapt themselves to the Egyptian way of life which surrounded them. That development figures prominently in Chapters 6 and 8. Here, meanwhile, as a preliminary example, we read of a man and woman who in all likelihood belong to the Graeco-Macedonian cleruchic milieu, adopting the Egyptian practice of trial cohabitation prior to formal marriage; the time is the middle of the second century.

Petition to the strategos of the Memphite nome from Ptolemaios son of Amadokos, Thracian. My mother Asklepias lived with a certain Isidoros, a resident of [the village of] Pitos pursuant to a memorandum of understanding which he drew up for her benefit. By its terms he acknowledged *inter alia* that he had received from her the dowry she brought worth two copper talents, and he undertook to present her with formal marriage lines within a year; that till then they were to live together as man and wife, exercising joint control over their property; and that if he did not do as written, he was forthwith to pay back the dowry with a 50 per cent penalty. [Within the year Asklepias died, followed by Isidoros, whose heirs seized the entire estate, refusing to return either the dowry or the loan that Ptolemaios had made to Isidoros, viz. 2,450 copper drachmas in principal plus 903 drachmas in interest. Hence Ptolemaios' petition for redress.][23]

Obviously there was, as we should expect, some intermarriage and some interpenetration of lifestyles. But the bulk of the evidence is equally clearly against any wholesale admission of Egyptians into the families and status of the Greek-speaking privileged class. The cleavage between the two ethnic groups, and the consciousness of their separateness, remained the dominant fact of socio-political life in Ptolemaic Egypt. While the restrictions on upward mobility succeeded in keeping the masses of the Egyptian population 'in their place', there were, besides intermarriage, two principal pathways by which some of them could attain higher status. Egyptians who acquired a working ability in the Greek language were needed in the local government bureaux, where their bilingualism created a communications bridge between the Egyptian-speaking populace and the Greek-speaking regime. From the mid-third century on, bilingual Egyptians are encountered not only in the lowly office of village clerk, but also occasionally in the nome-wide offices of royal secretary (for example Petosiris, p. 41) and finance officer. The next step up, to the office of nome strategos, who controlled military forces as well as civilian bureaux, was taken a few decades later, and before the end of the second century at least one Egyptian was able to rise to the eminence of epistrategos of the Thebaid. Appointees to these top-echelon posts were dignified with the lofty appellative of 'king's cousin', a piquant irony in the case of Egyptian incumbents. Significantly, such occasional advancement of Egyptians was confined to the internal administration of the country: not a single Egyptian has yet been found in the post of territorial governor in the Ptolemaic Empire abroad, or serving as ambassador or special envoy to any place outside Egypt.[24]

A military career provided the second, and broader, road to betterment of economic and social standing. It was only a matter of time before Egyptians had to be admitted to the military caste, some as mercenaries, others as cleruchs. In 217 BC a hurriedly assembled phalanx of 20,000 native Egyptians fought side by side with units of Graeco-Macedonians to repel a Syrian army poised to invade Egypt. Thereafter, especially as money was becoming tighter and foreign mercenaries a correspondingly more palpable drain upon the Treasury, the Ptolemies were driven to enrolling increasing numbers of Egyptians in the armed forces. For the government, that policy held out the promise of a double benefit: the natives' services were obtainable more cheaply than those of Greek mercenaries or cleruchs, and their accretion to the military ranks would broaden the base of the regime's support. The Ptolemies were careful, at the same time, to take measures aimed at preventing the Graeco-Macedonians from being too aggrieved at what might otherwise appear to be an equalization of status. They restricted severely the number of Egyptians admitted to officer rank or to the cavalry, which was more prestigious than the infantry, and, as mentioned earlier, they allotted to the Egyptian cleruchs landholdings that were significantly smaller in size than those of the Graeco-Macedonians.[25]

There are echoes in the sources also of other measures by which the regime now sought to emphasize the superior status of the Greek-descended soldiery. One such measure appears to have been the introduction of the term *katoikos*, 'colonist', to designate those of immigrant origin; but it was not long before the government found it necessary to admit at least some Egyptian cleruchs to that category as well. Another distinction which seems to have been more successful in excluding Egyptians was the *politeuma*. It is reasonable to suppose that from early on the Ptolemaic regime would seek to enhance the loyalty and *esprit de corps* of its military units, both professional and cleruchic, by stationing together men of common origin. In the second century, such groups were constituted as formal entities, which were called rather vaingloriously by the term which in the city-states of classical Greece had designated a government or body politic, *politeuma*. The essential function of a Ptolemaic *politeuma* was comparable to that which would be served today by a club for both officers and enlisted men. In addition, the *politeuma* afforded a convenient vehicle for executing administrative routines in the garrisons and cleruchies. The papyri mention *politeumata* of Boiotians, Cretans, and Idoumaians in Egypt, and there were doubtless others whose names have not been preserved. In the Ptolemaic overseas possessions, such as the island of Cyprus, we have evidence of comparable groups bearing the names of Achaians, Cretans, Ionians, Kilikians, Lykians, and Thracians. When there was no *politeuma* of fellow-expatriates to welcome a new entrant, the authorities would simply assign him an ethnic designation that would make him a member of an existing club. We know of one occasion, in the mid-second century BC, when 500 men were thus enrolled *en masse* in the *politeuma* of Cretans.[26]

In the world of the Greeks (and the Romans), social clubs were typically organized around the cult of a patron god or goddess. The rituals of that worship provided the membership with a calendar of festive days, which they celebrated together with the due rites and revels. The Ptolemaic *politeumata* adhered to that traditional pattern. What is more, they modelled themselves in their meetings on the assemblies of the Greek cities, electing officers, passing decrees, and going through other motions of self-government. This was, however, a social, not a political, autonomy.

Along with superior military rank and social position, the Graeco-Macedonian soldiery enjoyed a higher standard of living than the Egyptian. As already mentioned, the *klēros* of an immigrant settler normally fell in the range of twenty to a hundred arouras, while that of an Egyptian cleruch could be as small as five arouras and rarely exceeded thirty arouras. Particularly instructive in this regard is the land survey of 118 BC, preserved on a roll of papyrus over two metres long, from the office of the village clerk Menkhēs (Chapter 7). It lists first the lands held by 'the first- and second-category temples in the village', a total of $291\frac{7}{8}$ arouras, of which $150\frac{3}{8}$ were under cultivation. Those were lands whose revenues went, by royal grant or concession, to the priestly establishment to support the several cults, including those of the reigning and deceased sovereigns of the dynasty. The crown land, or royal domain administered directly by the government, amounted to $2,427\frac{19}{32}$ arouras, of which only $1,139\frac{1}{4}$ (or 47 per cent) were under cultivation; large areas had been abandoned by the peasants, the 'crown farmers' as the tenants were called, during the civil wars of the immediately preceding years. The cleruchic land amounted to something over 1,560 arouras (the figure for the total actually sown to crops is not preserved), itemized as follows:[27]

Holdings since the time of the king's grandfather [the names and patronyms that follow are Greek]:

Aphthonetos son of Hebdomaiōn	70 arouras
Pantauchos son of Pantauchos	34³⁄₃₂ arouras

Holdings since the time of the king's father:

[Four cleruchs with Greek names]	total = 124⅜ arouras

Holdings since the time of the king's brother:

[Seventeen cleruchs, four of whom have Egyptian names; one *klerōs* is held by two brothers jointly, another by a son in succession to his father]   total = 428⅞ arouras

Grants under the present king:

[Seventy-eight cleruchs; sixty-three of them, with Egyptian names, have holdings of up to nineteen arouras, perhaps thirty in one instance; those with Greek names hold ten to fifty arouras, two of them succeeding their fathers in the holding]   total = 924 arouras

As already remarked, many, if not most, Greeks who came to Egypt to be cleruchs had no intention of working the soil of their allotments with their own hands, meaning instead to lease out their holdings to others to farm while they enjoyed a *rentier*'s existence, often even living away from the land in a city or nome capital. Others came, tried their hand at farming, and decided that the *rentier*'s life was preferable. Successive generations in the second and first centuries came to regard themselves more and more as a kind of landed aristocracy, and less and less as soldiers. Reviewing the landholdings of 118 BC itemized just above, we find that only six of the thirty-three cleruchs with Greek names cultivated their land themselves; the rest leased out their holdings, in each case to a man or a woman with an Egyptian name. In contrast, only two of the Egyptian cleruchs leased their holdings to cultivators with Greek names.[28]

Even more significant was the evolution of the cleruchic landholding from an original lifetime tenancy to something approaching outright ownership. From earliest times, the history of Egypt was marked by a tug-of-war between the centripetal or unifying power of the monarch and the centrifugal or separatist forces of special-interest groups, foremost among them the rich and powerful priesthoods and the leaders of the military establishment, upon which the royal power was dependent. In the Hellenistic period the royal power and empire of Egypt were at their height under the first three Ptolemies (that is, to 221 BC). The long decline of the second and first centuries is reflected in the step-by-step progress of the cleruchs toward proprietary rights over the lands and lodgings assigned them.

In the beginning, when the system was instituted, the cleruch was granted only the usufruct of his *klēros*. The crown retained ownership, and once in a while we read of a cleruch ousted from his allotment for some infraction. Possession also reverted to the crown, at least in theory, when the cleruch's serviceability was terminated by death or disability. In reality, however, a superannuated or disabled cleruch would hardly be forced to surrender the landholding that provided his subsistence. The system would not long survive such demoralizing letter-of-the-law administration: how many cleruchs could the king have induced to sign on if they had to look forward, for themselves or their families, to such an unprotected, uncared-for old age? One saving provision that we know about granted a son the right to succeed to his father's cleruchic status. As early as the middle of the third century BC we have several examples of a *klēros* registered in the tax rolls in the name of an orphan. Details of the procedure for filial succession are preserved in an official document of 218 BC, in which the appropriate functionaries are notified, with regard to a cleruch who has died, 'to sequestrate the *klēros* in [the possession of] the king's Treasury, together with the yields of the current sowing, until it is registered as that of his sons, if he has any, within the number of days allowed by the statute'.[29]

A son enjoying such a peremptory right of succession is not far different from an heir apparent, and the cleruchy came increasingly to be regarded and treated as to all intents and purposes hereditary. In the document just cited, for example, it is said of the same *klēros* that 'the land belonged to him and his descendants'. Language such as this implies a right, or at least a privilege, of bequeathing and inheriting, and we have in fact, as early as 241 BC, an instance of a cleruch passing on his *klēros* by testamentary disposition. So too with the cleruch's lodgings. Like the land, his billet was officially the property of the crown. But in a will of 236/5 BC a soldier leaves to his son 'the lodgings which I received from the royal administration, and my horse and armour'. Equally or more significant is the will of the same year by which another soldier bequeaths 'my belongings and my lodgings' to his wife, a person who is obviously not in a position to assume his obligation of military service.[30]

In the following centuries, *klēroi* were freely disposed of by testament, and went to the next-of-kin if the cleruch died intestate. What is more, by the middle of the second century if not sooner, the *klēros* could pass to a minor, and by the first century to a daughter in the absence of a male heir. Nothing reveals more plainly how completely a *klēros* had come to be regarded as simply a family's landholding, how completely its possession ceased to be dependent upon the holder's availability for military service.[31]

Once the *klēros* was acknowledged to be heritable, that is, transferable within the family, the logical next step, which was not long in coming, was the admission of alienability, that is, allowing the *klēros* to be disposed of to someone outside the family. This further development probably came about somewhat as follows. From the start and increasingly thereafter, as we have already observed, cleruchs commonly leased their lands to others to farm. Once the practice of leasing was in effect, the resort to mortgaging would not lag far behind. Initially the land could be thus encumbered only with official permission and only within the cleruchic community, since foreclosure of a defaulted mortgage would entail the transfer of the *klēros* into hands other than those of the original assignee. But with time these restrictions became mere formalities, and eventually they became dead letters. A very recently published papyrus of 142 BC tells us of two cleruchs who exchanged landholdings in different parts of the Arsinoite nome. There is no suggestion that the transaction required any official permission; the authorities are asked only to verify that the boundaries of one of the parcels were in fact as represented by its transferer.[32]

The stage was thus set for the next step, namely allowing a *klēros* to pass into the possession of a non-cleruch, and that step too was taken, *de facto* if not always *de jure*, in the course of the second century. Instances now begin to appear where the holder-of-record of a *klēros* is someone other than a military reservist, sometimes even a woman. But some at least of those non-cleruchs must have felt a degree of insecurity, because they had acquired possession by a circumvention, if not an outright violation, of the letter of the law. Such holders were relieved of their uncertainty in 118 BC, the year in which Ptolemy VIII issued a series of amnesties and benevolences aimed at restoring tranquillity to an Egypt wracked by the civil war of the immediately preceding years. One edict guaranteed the legal tenure of all *klēros* holders who paid the rent or tax assessed on the land; no account would be taken of how they came into possession. Another edict was even more explicit: 'If cleruchs in financial straits have ceded or alienated their *klēros* . . . the tenure is guaranteed to the [new holders] and their descendants'. In short, a *klēros* could henceforth be transferred at will to, and acquired freely by, anyone. But interestingly enough, to the very end of Ptolemaic rule such transfers were always termed 'cessions', never 'sales'; the vocabulary of purchase and sale was carefully eschewed, thus avoiding any language impugning the crown's official ownership of the land.[33]

In this respect too, the disposition of cleruchic lodgings paralleled that of the land. In fact, these developments appear on present evidence to have begun with the billets and to have spread thereafter to encompass the land as well. A royal edict of 269 BC forbade 'obtaining a billet by cession or arranging it [privately] in any other way whatsoever'. But from 201 BC we have a deed by which a soldier, the son of a cleruch, cedes 'the lodgings belonging to his father'; and what is even more striking is that the transfer was made in that instance not to another cleruch, but to four Egyptians who were tenant-cultivators of crown land and had, to all appearances, no connection whatever with the military establishment.[34]

To close this chapter let us take note of two other benefits related to land, which soldiers and cleruchs of the Ptolemies enjoyed. One was that they were taxed at a much reduced rate on the produce of their landholdings; specific data along these lines will be found in Chapter 7. The second benefit, granted to many if not all, was exemption from special assessments, as in the following instance. The half-dozen years beginning with 170 BC were especially difficult ones for the Ptolemaic regime. With a boy-king (Ptolemy VI Philometor) on the throne, the Syrian ruler, Antiochos IV, seized the occasion to invade Egypt, the first successful entry of a hostile armed force into that land since Alexander the Great's sweep of 162 years earlier. Antiochos captured the young Ptolemy and proclaimed himself king of Egypt, but he was forced into an ignominious withdrawal by an ultimatum from Rome, now the rising power in the Mediterranean. (To the extent that the Roman senate can be said to have had a foreign policy in those days, it was to prevent the consolidation of any other first-rate power anywhere else in the Mediterranean.) Meanwhile, Antiochos' invasion had sparked a native revolt in the interior of Egypt, as a result of which extensive areas of farmland were devastated or abandoned. The effect was so severe that the restored government, in an effort to ensure against an inadequate food supply (which would have exacerbated the discontent still further), resorted for the first time to compulsory cultivation, that is, assigning to the farmers of each locality the parcels of idle land not voluntarily taken on lease by tenants. A papyrus roll in the Louvre gives us the details of that new imposition as ordered by the king's finance minister. A quantity of land was assigned 'to each according to his ability', but the order specifically exempted from such assignments 'the élite corps stationed in Alexandria, the seven-aroura and five-aroura [Egyptian] soldiers posted to [temporary] duty there . . . and the families [in the countryside] of those on duty in Alexandria'.[35]

2

The Engineer Kleon

Time: c.262–249 BC

Place: Arsinoite nome and adjacent regions (Map 2).

Documents: Among the many large finds made in the Fayyūm in the late 1880s by the noted archaeologist Sir Flinders Petrie was one of mummy cases fashioned of cartonnage—layers of papyrus plastered together into a thick cardboard-like casing, which was malleable when wet and remained rigid after drying. The constituent papyri, when separated, proved to contain a wide range of Greek documents of the third century BC, some fifty of which relate to Kleōn either as a private individual or in his official capacity. Known as the Petrie Papyri, the whole collection is divided among Trinity College, Dublin, the British Library, London, and the Bodleian Library, Oxford.

In the contemporary Zenon archive (p. 7) there is a reference to Kleon in a papyrus now in the Bodleian, and possibly another reference in a papyrus in the Cairo Museum.

Just when and whence Kleon came to Egypt are details that the papyri do not reveal to us. Clearly, however, he was one of the many trained professionals who poured into Ptolemaic Egypt, 'the land of opportunity', in the first great wave of immigration in the early decades of the third century BC. When we first encounter him, c.262 BC, Kleon is a man already well along in middle age, the father of two grown sons, Philonidēs and Polykratēs. His wife's name was Metrōdora.

The extant documents belong to the last decade or so of the years during which Kleon was, by royal appointment, a regional *architektōn*. The responsibilities of that office were much broader than those of a present-day architect. Kleon was, in fact, what we should call the chief engineer, or even the commissioner, in charge of the public works in his area. As such he was high enough up in the hierarchy of officialdom to be able to approach the king in person to request preferment for his sons when they were ready to enter upon their chosen careers. Two letters are worth quoting in that connection. The first, from a writer whose identity is lost, tells Kleon that:

your son Philonides, who has entrée to the king, brought presents including a beautiful gem-studded vase, and also a triton-shaped vase . . .

The second letter is to Kleon from his younger son, Polykrates, who has recently completed his training to be a surveyor.

Polykrates to his father, greeting. I trust you are well and everything is going satisfactorily; we too are well. I have written to you repeatedly to come here and introduce me [to the king], so that I may be rescued from my present state of unemployment. And so now again I ask, if it is possible and there is nothing in the public works to prevent you, try to come here for the festival of [the late queen] Arsinoē, for I am sure that commending me to the king will be easy if you are here in person. . . . Write us in reply, so we may know how you are and not worry [about you]. Take care of yourself to stay well and come to us in good health. Farewell.[1]

Both letters were written in Alexandria, where the sons lived and pursued their careers. It has generally been assumed that a man of Kleon's standing would also be domiciled in the capital, and that may well have been the case; certainly he began his career in Egypt there. But as his work in the years covered by the papyri kept him mostly in the field, some 300 kilometres up-river, he and Metrodora resided in those days in the 'county seat' of the nome, a town which the first Ptolemy named Krokodilopolis in honour of the Egyptian tutelary god of the region (and the name persisted even after the second Ptolemy renamed the town, along with the nome itself, for his queen Arsinoē after her death in 270 BC). Kleon's area of responsibility encompassed not only the whole Arsinoite nome, but also some adjacent territories in other nomes—the precise extent being dictated, presumably, by the needs of the works in hand. In the area under his purview, every relevant operation, from the provision of the raw

materials (such as the quarrying of stone) to the approval of
the completed project, was carried out under his orders and
supervision. He had a second-in-command named Theodoros,
to whom he would delegate some of his responsibilities (and
who in due course succeeded to Kleon's office), and at least
ten assistants whose duties corresponded more or less to those
of present-day foremen. His labour force of thousands, almost
entirely Egyptian, included not only masses of unskilled
manpower, but also artisans and craftsmen upon whose skills
he drew for the practical know-how empirically accumulated
by the native population over the pre-Ptolemaic millennia.[2]

According to the calculations of one scholar, Kleon's
income from salary plus allowances for food and expenses was
about 5,000 drachmas a year or more, some fifteen times what
a skilled worker would receive if he worked every day of the
year. In addition, there passed through Kleon's hands
impressively large sums of money and quantities of food, for
paying the many workers employed on the projects he
supervised. There is even a suggestion, as we shall see later,
that his accounts of these vast receipts and expenditures were
not always in the best order.[3]

The documents of the Kleon archive are particularly rich in
details about the irrigation works, both the new construction
and the never-ending tasks of maintenance and repair which
were required to keep the system operating at peak efficiency.
Such a system, designed to spread water from the Nile over
some of the land of the Fayyūm Depression (as we call it
today), had been introduced more than a thousand years
earlier by the Pharaohs of the Twelfth Dynasty. The
Ptolemies, in settling their cleruchs upon the land, aimed not
only at assuring that the allotments would be kept productive
but also at increasing the areas available for cultivation. In
many places the *klēroi* would be marked out so as to include
sizeable amounts of marginal, overgrown, or waste land,
which the holder would be encouraged to put into production
in order to increase his income. One general inducement
offered the cleruchs was a tax abatement. In the Arsinoite
nome this was combined with a public-works project conceived
on a grand scale, namely to upgrade the irrigation system of
the Pharaohs and extend it to serve large areas of newly

reclaimed land. Whether Kleon was involved in the devising of that ambitious design we shall probably never know. We do know that he was in charge of carrying it out, and we know some of the works he created, and some of the problems he faced in so doing.

The bottom of the Fayyūm Depression was, and is, permanently covered by a mass of water forming a lake, called Moeris in antiquity, Birket el Qurun today. By diverting some of the water flowing into it from the Nile, the Ptolemaic plan lowered the level of the lake (as archaeological excavations have revealed) by some eight to ten metres. In return, the land areas thus released from submersion had to be provided with irrigation water. That was done by constructing a number of large canals (a major one being named after Kleon), from which a network of feeder channels branched out over the entire area to be served. We read in Kleon's surviving papers about the construction of embankments, fascines, sluices, floodgates, jetties, and bridges. In a work-force including free men, slaves, and convicts, we encounter, among the skilled trades, quarrymen, masons, bricklayers, carpenters, blacksmiths, carters, and boatmen. In addition to these there were, of course, the hundreds of unskilled labourers engaged in moving and removing earth by digging, shovelling, and carrying. Some of the work was carried out under the direct supervision of Kleon and his staff, some was let to contractors. But the ultimate responsibility for satisfactory and timely performance of each undertaking lay with Kleon, and the completed works were subject to approval by government inspectors.

Once created, the irrigation network required regular maintenance. Here again the job might be let to a private contractor, who would hire the necessary labour; or else the state might requisition local manpower and animals to perform the necessary tasks. The following contract, from the time (as it happens) of Kleon's successor Theodoros, illustrates the first alternative. The long dating formula with which it begins corresponds to 8 October 245 BC, a time of the year when the Nile flood had just receded, leaving behind sizeable deposits of silt, a fertilizer for the fields but an obstruction in the irrigation channels.

In the reign of Ptolemy, son of Ptolemy and Arsinoë, sibling gods, year 2, Tlepolemos son of Artapates being priest of Alexander and the sibling gods, Ptolemaïs daughter of Thyïon being bearer of the sacred basket of Arsinoë Philadelphos, month Mesore the 21st, in Krokodilopolis of the Arsinoite nome. In the presence of the *architektōn* Theodōros and of Imouthēs from the office of Petosiris, the royal secretary [of the nome], a contract was awarded by the Treasury through the nome finance officer Hermaphilos to [two Greek names, imperfectly preserved] to clear out the sand from the irrigation channel at the canal near [the village of] Hephaistias to assure the irrigation of the land of the cleruchic cavalrymen, [beginning] alongside the boundary-stone of Timotheos' land and [continuing] for fifty *schoinia*. . . . [The contractors] will provide all their own equipment and will complete the work, without in any way obstructing the irrigation of the land, within thirty days from the day they receive the money. . . . They will receive half the money when the contract is signed and sealed and they furnish the [requisite] sureties. . . . When they have performed the work for the money [then] paid, they will receive the balance. If they do not do the work, or do not perform according to the contract, the official in charge shall have the right to re-award the work [and the defaulting contractors will be liable for damages].[4]

In the requisitioning of labour and supplies Kleon could likewise not proceed without the authorization of the appropriate government officials. Two of the letters in the archive will suffice to illustrate the point. The first is from Theodoros to the finance minister's representative for the region, where Theodoros finds he needs pack animals to transport material for strengthening the dikes. In the second, Kleon is instructed to requisition human labour to clear a channel which has become blocked by silt.

Theodoros to Diotimos, greeting. Please write most urgently to Androsthenēs and the nomarchs to send us, just as they did before, an authorization to requisition all the pack animals, as the river has reached all the dikes and they must be reinforced. [The date is lost.]

Alexandros to Kleon, greeting. In the overflow channel leading from Tebetnou and Samareia to Kerkeēsis, which we dug last year, silting-up has occurred. So please give orders to reduce the salt tax imposed upon the people of Kerkeēsis by 200 drachmas, which they will make up at the rate of 4 dr. for every 60 *aōilia* [of silt] that they remove, so that [the dredging] may be completed and the land not remain permanently flooded. Also, send us the rest of the 200 timbers (as long and as thick as possible, so that we may have them as joists for the bridges—we are being held up by [want of] them), likewise also 100 ropes, if you have more, 200. Goodbye. [Date, 7 August 254 BC][5]

This last letter is also one of several documents in the archive which reveal the kinds of pressures, the air of urgency, under which Kleon had to work much, perhaps most, of the time; he was, in effect, walking a tightrope between the demands or expectations of his superiors and the limitations of the possible. We get the impression that logistics were a constant problem, in particular assuring the timely delivery of supplies, so as to obviate or at least minimize delays in the work in hand. Likewise, the money for the payrolls and the food allowances had to be got to the work sites on time, or work stoppages might result. Aggrieved labourers in agriculture and industry alike had learned long before that downing tools and leaving the work site—in other words, going on strike— was their only effective recourse in the last resort. Often, in fear of reprisals, they would seek sanctuary in a temple, whence they could negotiate without facing arrest or physical violence.[6]

In addition to these typical everyday problems, Kleon experienced a whole series of difficulties stemming from a quite special source. In the middle decades of the third century BC an *éminence grise* hovered over the Arsinoite nome. He was Apollōnios the *dioikētēs*, or finance minister, the most powerful member of the king's 'cabinet'. Among the villages founded in the reign of Ptolemy II Philadelphos as settlements for cleruchs was one named Philadelphia, located on the north-eastern edge of the Fayyūm Depression. In the open-land area of Philadelphia the king bestowed upon Apollōnios an expanse of 10,000 arouras, the equivalent of some 6,800 acres, or 2,750 hectares.[7] Apollōnios hired a man named Zenon, a Greek from Asia Minor, to manage the estate for him, and Zenon's surviving papers, nearly 2,000 in number (p. 7), lay the estate's operations before us in minutest detail. While leaving the day-to-day operations to his resident manager, Apollōnios, though perforce engaged in Alexandria most of the time, kept in close touch with his Philadelphia estate and maintained a steady flow of instructions to Zenon and others, mainly by letters but also by frequent personal visits. Indulging in what we should call a flagrant conflict of interests, which his contemporaries obviously accepted as a matter of course, Appolonios repeatedly used his official position to advance his private interests in and around the estate. To realize Apollonios' expectations his local agents and subordinate officials often impinged upon Kleon's work with importunate demands for preferential treatment, thus aggravating his problems of manpower and supply. The following letters are typical. The first is from the man who preceded Zenon as Apollonios' estate manager. All the letters date from the period 11 October 257 to 11 July 255 BC.[8]

Panakestor to Kleon, greeting. We sent you word already on the 29th to send a crew to reconstruct the bends of the small canal. But you obviously just passed us by on your way to the small lake. Now, you shouldn't have passed us by but have come over for a while and inquired, when you saw that the land is unwatered, why we do not irrigate. For you have been appointed commissioner of works not only for the small lake but for here as well. So now at long last do come and meet us tomorrow at the sluice and direct what we must do to get the water past the bends, for we are inexperienced. We will provide you with the manpower and the rest of what you need, all that you order. But if you do not show up, we will be forced to write to Apollonios that in [all the Arsinoite nome] his land alone is not irrigated, even though we are willing to supply everything necessary. Goodbye.

Philoxenos and the other troubleshooters[?] to Kleon, greeting. The 140 quarrymen . . . are not working, because they do not have the necessities of life. As for the advance given them, they told us they have eaten that up, and now they are idle, with no one putting them to work. We therefore think it best for you to send them from the royal stores one artab of wheat each, so that they do not delay further, as the finance minister [Apollonios] is in a hurry for the housing. So all the quarrymen must be at their work. Goodbye.

To Kleon, greeting from the foremen of the quarrymen. We are ill used. What was agreed to by Apollonios the finance minister, none of it has come to us. Diotimos has the contract. Get a move on then, and see to it that Dionysios and Diotimos settle up with us in accordance with our contract, and the works do not come to a halt as has happened before. For if the workers learn that we have received nothing, they will pawn their tools.

No doubt Kleon had to face many such crises in the course of his career. That career, in fact, drew to a close only a few years after the time of the letters just quoted. In or about 252 BC the king visited the Arsinoite nome, and we learn from the Kleon archive that the irrigation works at the village of Ptolemais were not completed in time for the royal visit because of a shortage of boats to transport the quarried stone. In the case of some other unfinished works Kleon had been able to arrange temporary makeshifts, which did not, of course, conceal the fact that the work was unfinished. In this instance, it seems, his failure left an especially unfavourable impression. There are also some fragmentary remarks in some papyri which may suggest that the king's auditors now discovered some irregularities in Kleon's accounts. However that may be, it is clear that at about this time Kleon lost, or began to lose, the royal favour he had so long enjoyed. A letter from his wife, who had remained at home whilst Kleon accompanied the king on his inspection tour, tells us this in no uncertain terms. At some point in the tour, probably when signs of royal displeasure began to appear, Kleon wrote asking her to join him. Here is her reply:

You wanted to have me close to you, and I would have dropped everything and come there, but now I am frightened, and badly so, as I wonder how things are going to turn out for you and for us. The [king's] hunters, who arrived here this morning, told me what happened to you, that the king, on coming to the Lake [and seeing the unfinished work], raked you over the coals . . .[9]

It is also toward the end of Kleon's career that we should most reasonably place an undated letter in which Philonides, the elder son, urges his father to apply for retirement or, failing that, at least to take a temporary leave of absence and come to stay with him and his family for a while. The beginning of the letter is lost; what is preserved reads as follows:

. . . for in this way you will be able to obtain the king's favour again in the future. Absolutely nothing will be more important to me than to care for you for the rest of your life in a manner worthy of you and worthy of me, and to see to it, if something happens to you as it does to mortals, that you obtain all due respect. The most important thing to me will be to care for you, both as long as you live and when you have departed to the gods. So please make every effort to be released permanently, and if you find that is impossible, then at least for the duration of the river's ebb, when there is no danger [of flood damage], and besides you can leave Theodoros there to take over for you, so you can spend at least that time with us. Just bear in mind that you will experience no disgrace, and that everything will be seen to by me for your being free of pain and sorrow.[10]

Kleon did obtain a temporary leave; we know this from the following circular letter which a high official (not further identified) sent to the appropriate functionaries of the nome and the villages.

I am leaving Theodoros, the assistant *architektōn*, in charge of protecting the dikes and sluices, and I am also giving him authority over the earthworks of the dikes in the nome . . .[11]

As Theodoros is here styled 'the assistant *architektōn*', it is obvious that Kleon was still in office as Theodoros' superior. But not for much longer. Either the leave was extended into permanent retirement, or Kleon was otherwise induced to retire, or else he was simply relieved of his post. Documents beginning in or about 252 BC and continuing over the next fifteen years reveal that in those years the *architektōn* was Theodoros.

As for Kleon, with the letters just quoted he disappears completely from our view. We have no idea how much longer he lived, or what those years were like for him. Presumably he was allowed to retire with dignity; perhaps, as the relations between him and Theodoros appear always to have been good, he was even deferred to and consulted occasionally as the elder statesman. On the other hand, the note of concern in Philonides' letter makes it clear that there were plenty of envious characters around who were only too ready to publicize their delight at his fall from grace. But more we cannot say, and even much of this is speculative. There is no single scrap of evidence to break the silence of the sources on these matters.

3
Nikanor and Other Bankers

Time: 265–226 BC

Place: Oxyrhynchos and Lower Egypt.

Documents: The papers of the banker Nikanōr, dating from the 240s BC, constitute the smallest of the extant archives, thirteen papyri in all, half of them mere fragments. In order to fill out our picture of banking and bankers, the Nikanor papyri are supplemented in this chapter by other documents from the decades immediately preceding and following.

When their expanding economy reached the point of requiring the services of what we call a bank (probably in the sixth century BC) the Greeks simply used their word for 'table' to designate such a facility. (*Trapeza* is still today the Greek word for a bank.) The image is plain: the primitive bank was simply a table, or counter, across which goods and money changed hands.

By the Hellenistic age some banks had become enterprises of substantial size, engaging in a variety of services, both local and long-distance. Indeed, as evidence on the subject began to appear in the early papyrus publications of the turn of the century, enthusiastic writers professed to find in Ptolemaic Egypt the prototypes of the complex and sophisticated banking institutions and practices of modern times. Recent studies have backed away from such exaggerated notions, and their critical analyses of the much fuller data now available reveal that the activities of the Ptolemaic banks did not go much beyond the relatively simple transactions involved in receiving, paying out, and transferring money. They received tax payments deposited to the account of the Treasury, and paid out sums due from the state to civil servants, soldiers, religious authorities, tax farmers; they received and paid out money for private accounts; they acted as bureaux of exchange; and they loaned money on the security of land or precious objects. In the final analysis these are all implications, or variations, of the basic act of passing other people's money in and out.

Banks came into being in Egypt with the Ptolemaic regime, which introduced the money economy of the Hellenic world into an agrarian society geared essentially to barter. The papyri of the third century BC contain vivid evidence of the difficulties experienced by a bewildered peasantry learning to cope with the altered conditions dictated by the new, monetary, medium of exchange. An acuminous exposition of the underlying incompatibility between the two systems and populations is at hand from the pen of the eminent Belgian scholar to whom this book is dedicated, Jean Bingen. Analysing a long letter of 256 BC about an incident which precipitated a flight of peasants to the refuge of a temple, he wrote:

> The difficulty arose from the contact of two very different cultural states: on the one hand a peremptory dynamic of the [Greek] economy . . . and on the other hand the poorly organized peasants constituting, in the complex social structure of an Egypt in stagnation, a group particularly helpless in confronting the techniques of management, the techniques of money (which it does not handle), the dialectic of the Greek immigrant. . . . This conflict is probably representative of a certain number of problems of acculturation which presented themselves . . . after the installation of the Greeks in Egypt, problems which were never completely resolved.[1]

It was pointed out in Chapter 1 that the Ptolemies created a separate coinage, uniquely for domestic use. It was, and is, normal practice for a state to monopolize the issue of specie. The Ptolemaic government exercised something very close to monopolistic control over the operation of the banks as well. (The practical implications of this will appear in the next paragraph.) It is true that the expression 'private bank' does occur once, in a document from the very last decades of Ptolemaic rule, but the context of that occurrence is so bare that no firm deductions are possible. At a guess, one might suppose that the crown tolerated, perhaps even encouraged, the creation of privately owned banking institutions in those days of enfeebled royal power and straitened Treasury resources, days when Egypt was in effect a Roman protectorate

which Roman business men saw as a rich source of easy lucre.
But that was far into a future as yet unglimpsed in the mid-
third century BC, the time of the present chapter, a time when
Ptolemaic power was at its height at home and abroad.[2]

A quite recent (1981) study of banking in third-century
Ptolemaic Egypt distinguishes two categories of banks: royal
banks and concessionary banks. The former were, on present
evidence, by far the more numerous; indeed, they were
ubiquitous. They were operated under the supervision of civil
servants of the middle echelons, men who often served
simultaneously in other capacities as well. The concessionary
banks—apparently limited in number, but if so we do not
know on what basis—were leased out to the highest bidder, in
much the same way as the collection of certain taxes was
farmed out (p. 18): the successful bidder obtained a government contract allowing him to operate a bank in the locality or
region concerned.[3]

Beyond this administrative distinction the extant sources do
not reveal the differences between the two types of bank nearly
so clearly as we should like. The picture would be simple if the
banks were allocated discrete and mutually exclusive types
and areas of operation. On the contrary, however, there
appears to have been considerable overlap and duplication in
the kinds of transactions in which they engaged. Another
obstacle in the way of our obtaining a clearer understanding is
the fact that the extant evidence is rarely distinctive or
qualitative, but refers mainly to particular items of banking
activity; and as such items tend to be repetitive, differing
essentially only as to time, place, and the amount of money
involved, they fail to provide the materials necessary for any
comprehensive view of the banking system as a whole.

Most of the available evidence relates to the royal banks.
Let us begin at the fountainhead, Alexandria. All persons
arriving in Egypt from abroad had, as we saw in Chapter 1, to
exchange their foreign currency for the Ptolemaic before they
could even buy their next meal, let alone conduct any business
in the country. Did this imply the existence of a central 'Bank
of Egypt' in Alexandria? The evidence on that point is
inferential and ambiguous. It is obvious, however, that
Alexandria had one or more royal banks, as did the other

cities of the realm. In addition each 'metropolis', that is, each nome capital, had a royal bank to serve its nome, which it did with the aid of subsidiary branches established in some or all of the principal villages of the nome. The village branches are often referred to in the papyri as 'tax offices', presumably a popular rather than an official designation, indicative of their chief function in the experience of most people, that is as depositories for tax collections. The local branches were not, however, limited to that sole function. They also accepted private accounts, much as local post offices have done in our own times, and they were authorized to make loans, certainly to cleruchs, possibly to others as well.

The concessionary banks were introduced, on present evidence, in the reign of Ptolemy II Philadelphos. These banks, limited in number, are in evidence from *c*.260 BC. As far as we can now tell, they had nothing whatever to do with tax receipts, which were deposited exclusively in the royal banks. The concessionary banks, in other words, were confined to what we today call 'the private sector'. In addition to simple deposits and withdrawals, their customers could order payments to be made to third parties and funds to be transferred to banks in other places. The concessionary banks also served as exchange bureaux, and they made loans on security, for which they preferred, it appears, jewellery and other objects made of precious metals. In this last aspect they resemble a present-day pawnshop more than a present-day bank.

All the bankers whom we encounter in documents of the third century BC have names that are unmistakably Greek: Nikanōr, Pythōn, Artemidoros, Iasōn, Poseidonios, to mention but a few. Their clerks and assistants, however, especially those in the village branches, could be Egyptians—provided, of course, they had a command of Greek sufficient for the demands of the job. Here is the oath of office of such an assistant; it dates from *c*.230 BC.

In the reign of Ptolemy, son of Ptolemy and Arsinoë sibling gods, year . . . Epeiph 28. Oath sworn and subscribed by Semtheus son of Teōs, of Herakleopolis, assistant, also known as Herakleodoros. I swear by King Ptolemy son of King Ptolemy, and by Queen Berenikē, and by the sibling gods and the benefactor gods and their ancestors, and by Isis and Sarapis and all the other native gods and goddesses, that I will assuredly serve under Klitarchos, agent of the banker Asklepiadēs in charge of the branch office in [the village of] Phebikhis in the Kōite nome: I will duly and truly deposit all payments to the Treasury, and will deliver all money that I receive from Klitarchos, except for my salary, to the bank['s main office] in Herakleopolis; if any expenditure which I make in the field is authorized, I will give to Klitarchos an account of all payments, received and disbursed, and receipts for whatever I spend; if I owe anything [at the end of] my period of service, I will pay it to the royal bank within five days or execution for debt may be [made] upon me and all my possessions, and I shall not alienate anything of my possessions or this agreement shall be [evidence] against me, and I shall be available to Klitarchos and his agents outside sanctuary, altar, temple precinct and every [other] protection. If I abide by my oath, may it go well with me, if I violate my oath, may I be liable for sacrilege.[4]

Let us now look at some representative documents of banking activities, beginning with the papers of Nikanor, a banker in the metropolis of the Oxyrhynchite nome. Only six of the thirteen papyri surviving from his files are intact or sufficiently preserved to yield continuous sense. Most of them, as we shall see, havé to do with government funds kept in that bank. The earliest of them, bearing a date corresponding to 1 May 246 BC, is a receipt, written in duplicate, for salaries paid out from tax receipts. The next, of 20 April 245, is an official order authorizing a disbursement of that type. All are, in fact, largely self-explanatory.[5]

[Date.] Demetrios, physician, has received from Nikanor, banker of the bank in Oxyrhynchos, from the [revenues of the] medical account toward the sum still owed to the local physicians for the 39th year, the physicians' fee for Choiak of the 39th year [Jan.–Feb. 246], viz. 80 drachmas, which I have received in full from the banker.

Apollodotos [probably the police chief of the nome] to Nikanor, greeting. Pay to Theophilos, the guard assigned to duty by me at the bank, from the revenues of the police tax of the 39th year toward the maintenance money still owed the police chiefs, the maintenance money due for Choiak, Tybi and Mechir of the 2nd year [Jan.–April 245], i.e. 3 months, 600[+?] copper drachmas, and have him sign a receipt. [Date.]

Connections with government functions are seen also in the following.

[Date, 8 February 241.] Menodoros [a tax farmer] to Nikanor, greeting. Please write an order in my name to the bankers in the localities to give me the list of payers and payments toward the debits charged against me, so that I can use them to balance my accounts. Till now they have ignored me, and you yourself have not submitted it, although I have written repeatedly. I now therefore ask you again to write the order immediately. The cavalrymen are raising an enormous fuss and have cited me before Ammonios, the nome finance officer, but I am not authorized to guarantee their payments unless I get, either from you or from the bankers in the localities, the account of payments already made. Goodbye.

Diodoros to Pasikratēs, greeting. I have received from you for the Treasury, for the grain-purchase account of the Hermopolite nome, the sum paid out to me by Nikanor, the banker of the bank in Oxyrhynchos, pursuant to the letter written by you to him . . . fifteen copper talents (tal. 15). Goodbye. [Date, 21 January 241.]

Ammonios [the finance officer of the Oxyrhynchite nome] to Nikanor, greeting. Protarchos reports that you won't issue any papyrus rolls for [my office] unless I write to you who has [the authority to] receive them, so that you may conduct the transaction with him. Know, then, that . . . and give [my agent] Telestēs ten top-grade rolls and collect the price. . . . Goodbye. [Date, 31 January 241.]

Sixteen days later Ammonios wrote again, instructing Nikanor to 'give my agent Telestes for my office fifteen papyrus rolls'.

These letters from Ammonios bring us a valuable piece of new information about government operations. Banks, like all offices having to do with accounts, obviously used great quantities of writing materials. According to documents of 258/7 BC, the clerks keeping the accounts of the finance minister Apollonios during one of his inspection tours of Egypt consumed ten and even twenty rolls of papyrus a day, day after day. While we have no such statistic for Ammonios' office, or for Nikanor's, we can easily imagine that, with all the receipts the latter had to issue, all the records he had to keep, all the correspondence he conducted, he must have kept a storeroom well stocked with blank rolls of papyrus. And now we learn that from that store he filled not only his own needs but also those of such government offices as found it convenient to draw upon his supply.[6]

With tax revenues constantly pouring in and a great variety

of payments such as those noted above constantly going out, it seems likely that Nikanor's services to the state constituted the bulk of his bank's activity. Even so, that did not preclude his having private clients amongst the many inhabitants of the nome capital, whose convenience his bank could also serve. Here is a payment order relating to such a private account.

Ammonios to Nikanor, greeting. Pay from my account to Apollonios, agent of Antiochos, as the price of two calves, five hundred and forty copper drachmas. Goodbye. [Date, 9 February 241.]

[Added notation, probably Nikanor to his clerk] Pay cop. dr. 540.

Against the background just sketched, we should much enjoy examining how Nikanor kept his accounts, and the contents of some of them. None, unfortunately, have been preserved. Among the papers of Zenon (p. 42), Nikanor's contemporary, we do find some records that he kept of deposits and withdrawals or payouts. From these and other documents we see that the bankers provided their private customers with a variety of related services comparable to those available to the government offices.[7]

Here, for a first example, is a record of deposits, of *c.*258 BC. Gold, we see, commanded a bonus of 4 per cent when converted into silver.

100-dr. gold pieces, 15, plus conversion bonus
    of 60 dr.   [=1,560 dr.]
50-dr. gold pieces, 4,600 dr., plus conversion bonus of
    184 dr.   [=4,784 dr.]
60-dr. gold pieces, 85 = 5,100 dr., plus conversion bonus
    @ 6 dr. 4 ob. each = 566 dr. 4 ob.   [=5,666⅔ dr.]
Total = 2 tal. 10 dr. 4 ob.   [=12,010⅔ dr.]
Of this we withdrew 10 dr. 4 ob., leaving a balance of 2 tal.

It goes without saying that Zenon kept equally detailed records of expenditures. A simple example among the many is a papyrus (now at the University of Wisconsin) in which he itemizes each amount paid out by Artemidoros, the local banker, over a period of five months to twenty labourers hired by him for miscellaneous agricultural tasks—burning brush, digging ditches, cultivating, etc. Such unskilled labour was paid at the rate of ¾–1 obol a day, with boys assisting the men receiving only ½ obol, and the totals in this account amounted to 36 drachmas 4 obols one day, 16 drachmas 1½ obols another, and continued along in that order of magnitude. (Skilled labour at that time commanded up to a drachma [= 6 obols] a day.)

Bankers, of course, would not disburse any sum from any account without a written authorization. Here is another example of a routine payment order, followed by a letter revealing how the execution of such an order on a private account might be delayed by the priority enjoyed by the government accounts in the same bank.

Zenon to Artemidoros, greeting. Pay to Diodoros, clerk, his wages for [the month of] Phamenoth, 15 copper drachmas. Goodbye. [Date unclear.]

Ammonios to Zenon, greeting. In [response to your order] for withdrawal of 2,000 silver drachmas, we have given your agent Theodoros 1,000 in silver and copper. Iatroklēs and Theodoros will explain to you that we [intended to] send you the whole sum but could not because the soldiers arrived needing [money for] rations. Therefore please be so kind as to excuse us. Goodbye. [Date, 2 April 257.]

Zenon also kept a private account with a banker in Memphis, some sixty kilometres from Philadelphia. The first of the following selections is a letter from that banker. The second is a memorandum showing Zenon standing surety for a mortgage loan taken by his brother.

Poseidonios to Zenon, greeting. As you wrote me, I have given [your employee] Pyrōn the latest statement of your private account and pointed out to him the erroneous amounts of the discrepancy. He was detained here a few days because I was busy. Goodbye. [Date, 13 June 252.]

Pythōn, banker, [credited] to [the account of] Epharmostos son of Agreophōn, loan on mortgage of vineyard in Philadelphia in the sandy area, with Zenon son of Agreophon as surety, the mortgage on which has been recorded in favour of Diphilos son of Konōn, 3,700 copper drachmas. [Undated—no doubt a copy of the original.]

Zenon had accounts with bankers even farther away than Memphis. Python, of the mortgage memorandum just quoted, had his bank in Athribis, in the Nile Delta, as did Ammonios, the writer of the earlier letter apologizing for the delay in payment; Promēthiōn, whom we shall encounter in a moment, was located in the town of Mendēs, far up in the Delta, near the Mediterranean Sea. Beyond their basic function of receiving and disbursing funds, Zenon could also call upon any and all of them to assist and expedite his business dealings in their local markets. The first letter in the group now to be quoted is from a man employed by Zenon as a commercial traveller. It and the two following illustrate some of the services that Promethion was prepared to render his valued client, including (among others) the acquisition of papyrus rolls, that is, writing paper, a principal manufacture of the Delta region.

Molossos to Zenon, greeting. After I wrote you my first letter, which my man Horos took to you, Theogenēs arrived in Mendes on the 23rd with the three sealed bundles of flax that you had undertaken to furnish him [as samples]. They are selling here at . . . and the shopkeepers say, when questioned, that they can dispose of 10,000 bundles. Therefore, inasmuch as it is profitable for you, send someone as quickly as possible to arrange the deal, and order him to be careful to sell them at the greatest possible profit. Also write to Promethion the banker to help along, since it is his home territory. About the papyrus rolls I wrote you that . . . and when I ran into Kritōn in the Delta I asked him to tell you too. After you get that report, write me what to do and I'll see to it. And write to me about yourself, that you are in good health. Goodbye. [Date lost.]

Sōsos to Zenon, greeting. Sailing down to Mendes I delivered your letter and Iatrokles' to Dionysios and Promethion. As luck would have it, Apollonios the tax collector was there, so that Dionysios had that excuse [for delay], and as I stayed there ten days Promethion, excellent gentleman that he is, seeing me wasting several days there, gave me a letter to Diodotos in Alexandria to pay me 2,000 copper drachmas, and he said he had given Limnaios 1,200. So we are on the point of getting [all] the money. Goodbye. [Date, 23 January 250.]

Promethion to Zenon, greeting. I was distressed to hear that you have been in poor health for some time, but now that I hear you are better and are about ready to resume activity, I am happy. I too am well. As you wrote to me, I some time ago gave your agent Herakleidēs 150 silver drachmas from your account, and now he is bringing you 10 measures of myrrh in 21 alabaster containers which are sealed with my ring. Apollonios [the finance minister, Zenon's employer] wrote to me to buy and give him also garlands of pomegranate leaves, and we didn't give them to him before because they weren't ready, but they will be finished by tomorrow and will be delivered to him in Naukratis. The price of those and of the myrrh I have paid out from your account, as Apollonios wrote [to do]. I have also given 10 copper drachmas for [the freight charge of] the boat in which the myrrh is going up [the Nile to you]. There were also paid out to Iatrokles for the papyrus rolls being manufactured in Tanis for Apollonios 400 silver drachmas. Know, then, that these matters have been taken care of thus. And please write to me if you have any need of my services for anything. Goodbye. [Date, 20 February 256.]

We should very much like to know something about a banker's private life and social standing. On these subjects the extant documentation is totally silent; the papyri relating to bankers are all strictly business. All we can do is surmise that one whose business was handling large amounts of public and private funds could hardly have been, or long remained, a poor man himself.

4

The Strategos Diophanes

Time: 222–218 BC

Place: Arsinoite nome (Map 2).

Documents: Something over 125 Greek papyri, four of them in the British Library, London, the rest divided among the Cairo Museum and the Universities of Lille and Paris (Sorbonne). Two of the petitions from this archive have already been cited: see Chapter 1, notes 9 and 14. All these papyri were recovered from mummy cartonnage, which, upon being taken apart, was revealed to be composed of papyri discarded from the office of one Diophanēs. He, as the documents tell us, was stratēgos of the Arsinoite nome in the years 222–218 BC. He was probably in office longer than that, but those are the years to which the extant documents belong. What is more, at least eighty-eight of them, or more than two-thirds of the extant total, were acted upon and docketed in his office on the five days corresponding to 28 January 222 BC (twenty-one papyri), 26 and 27 February 221 (forty-one papyri), 13 January 218 (seventeen papyri), and 11 May 218 (nine papyri). No doubt some of the documents from which, in their damaged condition, the date is now missing, also belong to one or another of those groups.

Some 200 strategoi of Ptolemaic Egypt are known to us from the extant sources. Of them all, Diophanes is by far the best attested; that is, the number of extant documents addressed to or involving him in his official capacity far exceeds that available for any other Ptolemaic strategos.

The Greek word *stratēgos* means, literally, 'leader of an armed force'. When Alexander the Great overran the Persian Empire he replaced Persian governors, who were known as satraps, with men chosen from among his own military commanders, strategoi. Thereafter, governors of districts in the Hellenistic kingdoms of the eastern Mediterranean typically bore the title of strategos.

Here again most of our information—indeed, the overwhelming preponderance—comes from Egypt. Under the Pharaohs, the country was divided into about forty administrative districts. The Ptolemies retained the Pharaonic pattern in its essentials, designating the districts (now reduced in number, it would seem, but only slightly) as *nomoi*, a noun from the Greek verb meaning to 'distribute', or 'apportion'. The nomoi—or 'nomes' in our Anglicized form—have aptly been described as 'providing the framework for the life of their inhabitants. They were not only the organizational units of the regional administration, but also religious communities'.[1] The cult in each nome centred on the worship of a tutelary animal god—ibis, crocodile, etc. Each nome was governed by a strategos, who was appointed by the king and remained in office at the royal pleasure. The strategos headed the civil government of the nome and exercised command over the military forces, including cleruchs, stationed there to assure the public tranquillity.

Diophanes' name tells us that his forebears were Greek or Macedonians. (This in turn illustrates the policy of the first Ptolemies with regard to the higher administrative offices: not until the middle of the second century BC do men with native Egyptian names begin to appear in the office of strategos.) The extant papyri tell us nothing further about Diophanes' background, nor about his activities as military commander. That is because the documents of the archive were all submitted to his office by individuals seeking redress of private grievances. Consequently, we encounter Diophanes only in his non-military capacity, only in the exercise of his administrative, judicial, and police authority. Still, the variety of the complaints that we find in the papyri from his office makes the Diophanes archive a veritable kaleidoscope of the bustling life in the villages and capital city of the nome.

About a dozen of the documents in the archive survive as mere fragments, too small for a clear determination of their original nature. Of the rest, the overwhelming majority are complaints seeking the recovery of money or property; twenty, at most, might be classified as seeking criminal penalties.

Petitions for redress were addressed pro forma to the king, among whose officially proclaimed attributes were those of protector of his people and dispenser of boons and justice. These petitions were actually delivered, however, to the office of the nome strategos, and they went no higher up the administrative ladder; they were acted upon in the strategos' office itself. In rare and special instances a petition might perhaps be reserved for the strategos' own eyes, but the normal procedure, as we can reconstruct it from the evidence of the documents, ran more or less as follows. The strategos would listen as one of his clerks read the complaint aloud. He would then dictate a brief instruction, which was scribbled at the bottom of the petition by the clerk. We cannot help wondering whether the point was ever reached where, in routine matters, the clerk was authorized to append the instruction without bothering the strategos. On this subject there is no solid evidence either way, but the appearance of the documents would seem to argue against such a supposition.

Once acted upon by the strategos (or in his name) the petition was retained for filing in his office, but a copy of the whole, petition plus instruction, would be handed to the petitioner to deliver to the official to whom the instruction was addressed, usually the police chief of the village in which the accused resided. Whether that copy was prepared in the strategos' office or was provided by the complainant's being required to submit his petition in duplicate, is not clear. Perhaps the petitioner was given a choice: submit in duplicate, or pay a fee to have the duplicate prepared by a clerk in the strategos' office. At all events, the papyri that constitute our Diophanes archive are the copies that were retained in the strategos' office; eventually, when no longer needed, they were discarded by that office and acquired by a coffin-maker to be used in making papyrus cartonnage.

Whether stemming from government policy, from personal inclination, or from some combination of both, Diophanes' handling of the complaints presented to him shows that he preferred the role of peacemaker to that of inflictor of punishments. The principal leitmotif running through his instructions scribbled at the bottom of the petitions is: don't litigate, settle. Calm them down and reconcile them if possible, he usually tells the police chief. The weight of such an order from the highest official in the nome, delegated by the king himself, was no doubt sufficient, in many cases, to pressure the parties into settling their differences 'out of court'. Only when that approach failed to terminate the dispute would Diophanes be faced with the necessity of deciding the matter himself or referring it to the appropriate tribunal.

In his instructions to the local police Diophanes employed some half-dozen formulae, of which the following were the most common.

   1. 'If at all possible reconcile them. But if not, send him/her/them to me so I can look into it' (*or:* 'so that he/she/they may be judged in the appropriate court'). This is by far the most frequent instruction, occurring at least forty times, which is to say in a third of the cases. In one instance, where an Egyptian bath attendant is charged with scalding a Greek woman, this formula is reduced to a brusque, 'Send the accused to me.'[2]
   2. 'Look into it and see that he/she obtains justice.' Diophanes used this formula for minor matters, matters which he felt could be left entirely to the discretion of the police chief. Presumably the latter, if he hit a snag, could still refer the matter back to the strategos.
   3. 'Look into the law, and make them do what's right. If they object, send them to me.'
   4. 'Fill me in on what this is about.'

These formulae were so standard, so familiar, that the clerks, bored by the monotony of the routine, reduced their writing of these instructions—at least in the copies being retained in their files—to a bare minimum, and sometimes (to us, at least) even less than that. Typically they wrote, in a tiny scrawl, something approximating to the first letters of each word and a mere squiggle or two to represent the rest, in much the way many people sign their names these days. In a few instances, the array of strokes, stabs, and squiggles is so crabbed and forbidding that the decipherment of the instruction, in spite of familiarity with the formulae, remains far from certain.

Reading through the documents of the Diophanes archive, the social historian quickly becomes aware that quite often the dispute submitted to the strategos pits Egyptian against Greek. This is the case in twenty-five papyri, a fifth of the archive. In eighteen of those twenty-five (72 per cent) the complainant is a Greek, in the other seven instances the situation is reversed. The grievances concern mostly damage to property, quarrels over lodgings, failure to deliver paid-for goods, failure to repay loans, and assault and battery. This last group, ten in number, affords an illustration of the pervasive, mutual hostility between the two populations. Compounded of Greek disdain for the indigenes and Egyptian resentment of ill treatment by their overlords, that hostility simmered close to the surface of their daily intercourse, ready to erupt into violence at even slight provocation. In three of the ten complaints of physical violence we find Greeks accusing Greeks, in one it is an Egyptian woman against another Egyptian woman, in one it is an Egyptian against a Greek, and in all the rest Greeks complain against Egyptians. Here are typical examples.

To King Ptolemy greeting from Pasis, a[n Egyptian] farmer of Polydeukia. I am wronged by Geroros, a [Greek] holder of seventy arouras. I own a house in the village, and I have been thrown out by him by force together with my cattle, which are [wandering loose] in the open air, even though he has a place in the village that was given to him as his lodgings. I therefore, beg you, O king, if it please you, to instruct Diophanes the strategos to write to Sosibios the police chief to order the man sent up to him, and, if what I say here is true, not to allow him to throw me out of my own house, so that I may be able to attend to my farming and through you, O king, the common saviour of all, I may obtain justice. Farewell.
[From Diophanes] To Sosibios: If at all possible reconcile them. But if not, send them over to be judged by the mixed [Greek–Egyptian] tribunal. [Date, 26 February 221 BC.]

To King Ptolemy greeting from Tetosiris [an Egyptian woman]. I have a lawsuit pending . . . against Apollodoros [a Greek] over a house located in Berenikē Thesmophorou. Needing witnesses for the trial, I obtained from the clerk of the court a letter instructing the police chief, Herakleodoros, to take sworn depositions from the witnesses I would bring to him. Apollodoros, bringing a gang[?] with him, burst in and terrorized all my witnesses, saying he would beat them and me within an inch of our lives and drive us out of the village. He even abused Biou——, a [Greek] hundred-aroura holder

who was going to give evidence for me, and said he would beat him
up too, for which reason he did not give evidence for me. As the
others who were going to give evidence for me are Egyptians, they
were intimidated and took to their heels and did not give evidence. I
therefore ask and beg you, O king, not to allow justice to be delayed
thereby . . . but to instruct Diophanes the strategos to write to
Herakleodoros to send up to Diophanes those who, as I will inform
him, built this house—hod carriers, carpenters, masons[?]—so that
he may take their sworn depositions . . . and when that has been
done I, O king, fleeing for refuge to you, the common benefactor of
all, will experience your benevolence. Farewell.

To King Ptolemy greeting from Herakleidēs, originating from Alexandros' Isle, now residing in Krokodilopolis in the Arsinoite nome. I
am wronged by Psenobastis, who lives in Psya, in the aforesaid
nome. On Phamenoth 21 of year 5 in the fiscal calendar, I went to
Pysa in the said nome on a personal matter. As I was passing by [her
house] an Egyptian woman, whose name is said to be Psenobastis,
leaned out [of a window] and emptied a chamber pot of urine over
my clothes, so that I was completely drenched. When I angrily
reproached her, she hurled abuse at me. When I responded in kind,
Psenobastis with her own right hand pulled the fold of my cloak in
which I was wrapped, tore it and ripped it off me, so that my chest
was laid quite bare. She also spat in my face, in the presence of
several people whom I called to witness. The acts that I charge her
with committing are: resorting to violence against me and being the
one to start [the fracas] by laying her hands on me unlawfully.
When some of the bystanders reproached her for what she had done,
she simply left me and went back into the house from which she had
poured the urine down on me. I therefore beg you, O king, if it
please you, not to ignore my being thus, for no reason, manhandled
by an Egyptian woman, whereas I am a Greek and a visitor, but to
order Diophanes the strategos . . . to write to Sōgenēs the police chief
to send Psenobastis to him to be questioned on my complaint and to
suffer, if what I say here is true, the punishment that the strategos
decrees. Farewell.[3]

Theft and damage to property were other common complaints. These, in noteworthy contrast to those charging
physical violence, are mostly complaints of Greek against
Greek or Egyptian against Egyptian. Such a finding is really
not surprising. Rather, it is but a faithful reflection of the
degree to which the two population groups went about their
daily lives, as far as possible, in two discrete circles. They

were, none the less, living in close proximity, and inevitably disputes of this kind also crossed ethnic lines, as in the following complaint of a Greek against two Egyptians.

To King Ptolemy greeting from Idomeneus, farmer on the estate of Chrysermos, of the village of Kaminoi. I am wronged by Petobastis son of Taōs and Hōros son of Keleēsis, of the same village. I am the lessee of two arouras in the estate of Chrysermos, and after I had planted the land to chickling, Petobastis and Horos flooded my field, washing out the seed, so that my chickling is a total loss and I cannot even recover my out-of-pocket expenditures on the land. I therefore beg you, O king, if it please you, to instruct Diophanes the strategos to write to Hephaistion the police chief to send Petobastis and Horos, the accused, to Krokodilopolis so my case against them may be judged by Diophanes; and if I demonstrate that they flooded and washed out my sown field, [I beg] that they be compelled to take over my field and pay the rent, and that I be given out of the land that they farm an equal tract in exchange for the one they flooded. When that is done, fleeing for refuge to you, O king, I shall be able to pay my rent to Chrysermos, and I shall have experienced your benevolence. Farewell.
[From Diophanes] To Hephaistion: If at all possible, reconcile them. But if not, send them over after [the 24th], to be judged in the appropriate court. [Date, 13 January 218.][4]

The following are examples of complaints of thefts and unpaid debts. All three incidents occurred within the Greek-speaking community, and in the second case the dispute is even an intra-familial one.

To King Ptolemy greeting from Sosigenēs, of [the village of] Theogonis. I am wronged by Hippoïtas, of [the village of] Berenikis Thesmophorou. On Tybi 18th [69 days ago] one Demetrios, a Syrian who happened then to be living at Theogonis, made off with property of mine worth 154½ drachmas. He then appeared in Berenikis Thesmophorou, where he was discovered by the aforesaid Hippoïtas, who arrested him and seized a copper goblet and twelve copper drachmas which were part of the loot. After his arrest Demetrios, interrogated by Herakleides the police sergeant[?], acknowledged that he had given Hippoïtas the goblet and the twelve drachmas, whereupon Herakleides ordered him to give me back the goblet and the twelve drachmas. He has indeed given me back the goblet, but not the twelve drachmas. I therefore beg you, O king, to instruct Diophanes the strategos, to write to Mikōn the police chief to send

Hippoïtas, since he is no longer a policeman, to Diophanes and, if it is as I write, to compel him to give me back the twelve drachmas. When that happens, through you, O king, I will obtain justice. Farewell.

[From Diophanes] To Mikon: Look into it and see that he obtains justice. [Date, 11 May 218.]

To King Ptolemy greeting from Theōn and Teutios, sons of Philippos, Macedonians by descendance, of [the village of] Pharbaithos. We are wronged by Theudotos and Agathōn, who are relatives of the late Philippos' mother. As guardians of Philippē, daughter of Philippos, we were looking for certain items of property bequeathed by Philippos and we discovered that the aforesaid persons took away some of them, which we will itemize before Philotas the police chief. Also, as we needed twenty-five drachmas for Philippos' funeral we pawned his cuirass and tunic, and his cloak together with its packing-case, with the said Agathon. But now that we want to redeem those objects by paying the sum lent on them plus the interest, he won't give them up but keeps delaying. We therefore beg you, O king, if it pleases you, to instruct Diophanes the strategos to write to Philotas the police chief so that, if what is written in this petition is true, Philotas may compel Theudotos and Agathon to give us back the items—of which we will supply a list—that they took away, and Agathon to accept the principal and interest and give us back the pawned items. Thus, fleeing for refuge to you, O king, the common succour and benefactor of all, we will obtain justice and the orphan girl will not suffer injustice. Farewell.

[From Diophanes] To Philotas: If at all possible, reconcile them. But if not, send them to us after [the 24th] to be judged in the appropriate court. [Date, 13 January 218.]

To King Ptolemy greeting from Alexandros son of Peith——, of [the village of] Pharbaithos in the Herakleidēs division [of the Arsinoite nome]. I am wronged by Apollonios son of——. [Over two years ago] when I leased a market garden from Theugenēs [who had leased it from the crown], I gave Apollonios twenty drachmas, the rental of the garden, to pay into the bank. He paid in ten drachmas but continues to delay the other ten and even now he still has not paid them into the bank. Now Theugenes, the holder of the property, is demanding from me in accordance with my contract with him the sum plus [overtime] interest and a penalty of half, since Theugenes had to pay the bank the ten drachmas himself. I therefore beg you, O king, if it please you, to instruct Diophanes the strategos to write to [name lost] the police chief to send Apollonios to be judged in my complaint against him and, if what I say here is true, that I may collect from him the ten drachmas plus the additions demanded of me [by Theugenes], so that, fleeing for refuge to you, O king, I may obtain justice. Farewell.

[From Diophanes] To——: Look into it and see that he obtains justice. [Date, 28 January 222.][5]

As this last petition reveals, failure to repay a debt on time subjected the debtor to a 50 per cent penalty in addition to a continued piling-up of the interest. The consequences could be even more serious, namely, confinement in a debtors' prison. As the Diophanes archive contains no example of a debtor who suffered such imprisonment, let us digress for a moment to quote the following report sent by a village police chief, no doubt to his strategos; it dates from a few decades later than the Diophanes archive.

On Phaophi 7 of the 6th year Hermias son of Dagouzis, a resident of the said village, handed me a memorandum against Khenephibis son of Herieus and his wife Taarmotis daughter of Pasis, to the effect that, owing him pursuant to a six-witness contract 6 artabs of wheat, they had paid him neither those nor the 50 per cent penalty on them, and he asked that they be summoned to pay him back the wheat and the penalty. On the 8th of the said month I summoned Khenephibis, and when he acknowledged [his indebtedness] I turned him over [to be held in custody] till he did what was right.[6]

Claims for overdue payments appear frequently in the petitions to Diophanes. The claims stem from contracts of all sorts—sales, leases, loans, employment. Some representative cases follow; the first is particularly interesting because it introduces us to two of the minority groups living in Egypt, the accused being, to judge by his name, a Syrian, and the petitioner belonging to a group of Arab settlers.

To King Ptolemy greeting from Paratēs, Arab, barber, inhabitant of [the village of] Ptolemais-of-the-Arabs. I am wronged by Malichos son of——sazaios. For some years now I have rendered my services to him and his family, practising my calling in customary and irreproachable fashion, in return for a salary agreed upon between Malichos and me. But now [he hasn't paid me for] the past year and, disputing my [claim], he made me go to the temple of Athena and swear that I had in truth not received it. . . . I beg you, O king, not to ignore the injustice done to me, a man who lives by his calling, but to instruct Diophanes the strategos to write to Ptolemaios the police chief [to verify] if in fact I have sworn the oath as he demanded, and if he is willing at long last to pay my claim; and if he demurs at all, to send him to Diophanes. When that is done, O king, I shall have experienced your benevolence. Farewell.

[From Diophanes] To Ptolemaios: If at all possible, reconcile them. But if not, send them over to be judged in the appropriate court. [Date, 26 February 221.]

To King Ptolemy greeting from Dioskouridēs and Nikanōr [Greeks]. We are wronged by Nephersoukhis [an Egyptian]. Having borrowed from us [a few months ago] ten copper drachmas from Dioskourides and fourteen copper drachmas from Nikanor, for a total of twenty-four drachmas, she doesn't pay it back, as she has gone off to Kerkesoukha in the Herakleidēs division and thinks nothing of us. We therefore beg you, O king, if it please you, to instruct Diophanes the strategos to write to Deinias the police chief of Kerkesoukha to summon her, and if she acknowledges [the debt] to collect the money from her and pay it over to us, or if she denies it, to send her to Diophanes the strategos, so that we may experience your benevolence. Farewell.

[From Diophanes] To Deinias: If at all possible, reconcile them. But if not, send her over so they can be judged before the mixed tribunal. [Date, 26 February 221.]

To King Ptolemy greeting from Marōn son of Euktos, Argive by descendance. I am wronged by Theodosios son of Xanthos, Lykian by descendance. My son Euktos took from Artemōn, jointly with Theodosios, a ninety-nine-year lease on a building site in [the village of] Autodikē, but he died before they divided the site and Theodosios marched in and erected the walls of a dwelling, choosing the most desirable and most accessible spot. Thereafter a division was arranged, and although the agreement specifies an equal and comparable division, he did not share with me justly but cheated me, giving me a useless lot, long and narrow, while keeping his own lot square. I therefore beg you, O king, if it pleases you, to instruct Diophanes the strategos to write to Pythiadēs the police chief to go to the site and divide it so my lot is equal and comparable, and also to make him remove to his own part the half-finished doorway which he erected in my part, and, as he has intruded seventy square cubits on me, to make him give me in exchange an ingress and egress to our common street, since I have been pushed farther back. When that has been done, through you, O king, I shall have obtained justice. Farewell.

[From Diophanes] To Pythiades: If at all possible, reconcile them. But if not, send them to us after [the 24th] to be judged in the appropriate court. [Date, 13 January 218.][7]

Domestic quarrels constitute still another group of complaints submitted to Diophanes. The above-quoted petition regarding the property of the orphan Philippē is one example. Of the following cases the first, involving a father, a prodigal son, and a prostitute, reminds us that those stock characters and situations of the Hellenistic stage were rooted in reality. The plays of Menander and other writers of the New Comedy were set in Athens and other cities of the Greek homeland; our setting is the capital of the Arsinoite nome, where the sizeable population of Greek immigrants and their descendants energetically created and strove to preserve for themselves a milieu and way of life as close to those of their homeland as possible. In the second of the following petitions, also involving members of the Greek community, an aged father complains that his son has failed to provide promised support.

To King Ptolemy greeting from Sopolis. I am wronged by a certain Demō, who resides in Krokodilopolis in the Arsinoite nome and is a prostitute. With the help of some men she induced my son Sopolis, who is still a minor, to sign a promissory note for a loan of 1,000 drachmas from her. I therefore beg you, O king, if it please you, to instruct Diophanes the strategos to summon Demō and the man whose name appears on the note as her legal representative, and the keeper of contracts, so that he may interrogate them unsparingly and, if it is revealed that in no wise did a loan of money take place but the document was drawn up for a fraudulent purpose, that he may compel her to hand over the note to me and may pronounce judgement regarding her. When that is done, O king, I will be rescued from injustice, I who have furnished my services to you and your father in blameless fashion. Farewell.
[Office notation] Demetrios son of Nikagoras was delegated [to handle the matter]. [Date, 27 February 221.]

To King Ptolemy greeting from Pappos. I am wronged by Strouthos, my son. I sent him to school and gave him a good education. When I grew old and could not provide my own subsistence, I appeared[?] in the village of Arsinoē before Dioskouridēs, your deputy[?], who ordered him to furnish me with one artab of wheat and four drachmas per month, in which terms Strouthos himself concurred. But despite that he has given me nothing of what was agreed to, and whenever he meets me he abuses me most shamefully. What is more, he forces his way into my house and each time he makes off with whatever piece of houseware is handy, disregarding me because I am old and losing my sight. I therefore beg you, O king, to instruct Diophanes the strategos to write to the police chief of the village of Arsinoë-on-the-Dike, in the Themistēs division [of the nome], to send Strouthos to Diophanes who, if what I say in this petition is true, can restrain him from violence and make him furnish sureties for my pension, so that he will pay it regularly in the future. When that is done, through you, O king, I shall have obtained justice. Farewell.

[From Diophanes] To Ptolemaios: If at all possible, you yourself reconcile the father with Strouthos. But if he demurs at all, send him over to me, and I will see that it works out in no other way. [Date, 21 November 222.]

[Notation on back] Strouthos appeared [before Ptolemaios] and said he would give Pappos two copper drachmas a month for his subsistence. Pappos was present and said he was satisfied with those terms.[8]

Although eight of the petitions in the archive have such office notations indicating the action taken by the police chief and its result, only the one just quoted is well enough preserved for decipherment. But there are also several papyri containing brief messages sent to Diophanes by police chiefs reporting what they had done in response to his instructions. Here is a typical example:

Demetrios to Diophanes, greeting. Epistratos, a 'descendant' living at Mouchis, brought me his petition against the farmers regarding [damage caused by] their burning off brush—a petition on which your notation instructs me if at all possible to reconcile them, but if not to send them over to you to be judged in the appropriate court. So then, I summoned the farmers living in the village and read them the complaint, but as they reject conciliation at my instance I have sent them over to you, and I write so to inform you.

Another document illustrates a different element in the procedures adopted, namely the taking of sworn depositions. Here is the same police chief reporting to Diophanes; once again, it is a case of Egyptians against Greeks.

You wrote me to take sworn depositions from the witnesses produced

by Horos and his brothers for their case against Ptolemaios and
Zopyros. I have certified their depositions and send them to you
[herewith], sealed with a stamp whose device is a face of Helios. I
also append for you[r information] the names of the deponent witnesses.
Against Zopyros: [twelve names are listed, all Egyptian]
Against Ptolemaios: [the same names].[9]

It is unfortunate that nothing in the archive helps us to
discover whether or not a police chief was generally able to
settle the complaints referred to him. A priori we should think
so; else why would the strategos make such referrals his
normal procedure? In addition, as the disputant parties knew
the police chief to be acting with authority delegated by the
strategos, we might suppose that they would normally accede
to his arbitration; but it must be admitted that there is little
hard evidence to support either that or the opposite inference.
The extant documents of the type just quoted reveal that the
police chief's intervention was sometimes successful, sometimes not. What we do see clearly or sense, in one case after
another, is that the life of the villages in which cleruchs were
settled was pervaded by a gnawing, corrosive spirit of mutual
antipathy, by feelings of resentment and distrust—and yes,
even fear—which characterized the attitudes of the Greek élite
and the Egyptian underclass for each other. Expressions of
that hostility—in physical assaults, in property damage, in
broken contracts—have met us on almost every page of this
chapter, and will reappear repeatedly in the chapters that
follow.

5

The Recluse Ptolemaios

Time: 164–151 BC

Place: The sanctuary of Serapis, just west of Memphis.

Documents: A little over a hundred Greek and some Demotic papyri. The Greek papyri, scattered among a dozen or so different collections, were given a truly monumental re-edition, with an extraordinarily exhaustive commentary, by U. Wilcken, *Urkunden der Ptolemäerzeit* (hereafter *UPZ*), vol. I (Berlin and Leipzig, 1927).

The Serapeion

Memphis was the Pharaonic capital of Lower Egypt, as Thebes was of Upper Egypt. On the outskirts of Memphis, by the desert's edge, there grew up from earliest historical times a great religious complex for the worship of the major and many of the minor gods of Lower Egypt. At present-day Karnak we can still see the awesome remains of the temple complex that was built just outside Thebes by a succession of Pharaohs. In contrast, the ruins found by the nineteenth-century excavators at Memphis are pitifully slight, but even so they are enough to indicate the vast extent of what once was there.

The earliest worship at Memphis was a cult of the bull, Apis. Before long, that became associated with the cult of Osiris, and the godhead became known as Osiris-Apis, or Oserapis. This was the obvious source of the name Serapis—or Sarapis, both spellings were common—the name chosen by Ptolemy I for the politically inspired Egypto-Hellenic cult figure that he created in or about 286 BC. His choice was dictated, or at least influenced, also by the fact that the Memphis shrine had been growing in importance for some time, most notably as the therapeutic centre we shall be looking at presently.

After the creation of the Serapis cult the Ptolemies rebuilt and expanded the sanctuary at Memphis on a lavish scale, and thereafter it was generally referred to as 'The Great Serapeion', or 'The Great Serapeion at Memphis'.[1] In Greek and Egyptian milieux alike, the god Serapis was an instant and enduring success, one that lasted all through antiquity until the triumph of Christianity, even though the Egyptians never came even close to the status of equality with the Greeks that Serapis was supposed to symbolize. For them that symbol remained no more than an ideal in a hoped-for future, never becoming a present reality. In fact, there were really two separate cults of Serapis: the Greeks worshipped him with the rituals of a Greek god, often portraying him in one of the guises of Zeus, while the Egyptians treated him entirely as one of their own.

In the worship of Serapis at Memphis we see him consulted as an oracle; appealed to as protector from troubles, rescuer from dangers, and dispenser of justice; and invoked as ruler of the universe, 'greatest of the gods', to grant the royal house 'health, victory, power, might, and rule over all the lands under the heavens'.[2]

The complex of buildings at The Great Serapeion included shrines of several other gods, some closely, others loosely, associated with the Serapis cult. The description of the Serapeion at Alexandria in a recent book can serve us as a thumbnail sketch of the Memphis sanctuary as well: it 'was a large open sacred area with corridors, subterranean crypts, and a labyrinth of shrines . . . An army of divinities, Greek and Egyptian, crowded into the [precinct], all of them related in one way or another to Serapis, Isis, or Harpocrates'.[3]

The most important of the associate divinities at the Serapeion was Isis, she of the hundred attributes, including those of giver of life and helper in troubles. She was invoked along with Serapis in the prayers for Ptolemaic world rule. The temple personnel performed her rites and celebrated her festivals. In fact, in the archive explored in this chapter there are discernible signs that by the third century BC the Isis cult had already begun the rise in prominence that was to result in the centuries-long vogue which it later enjoyed throughout the Mediterranean world.

Of the lesser gods whom we find 'in residence' in The Great

Serapeion, the one that drew the greatest numbers of pilgrims
and suppliants was the Egyptian Imhotep, whom the Greeks
identified with their Asklēpios, the healing god. The fame of
this cult spread far beyond the confines of the Ptolemaic
Empire, and in the outside world the whole sanctuary was
often referred to as 'The Great Asklepieion at Memphis'.

Like its progenitors in Greece, of which the best known was
the world-famous shrine at Epidauros, the Asklepios cult at
Memphis attracted streams of invalids who came hoping that
the god would cure them of their illnesses and infirmities. The
ritual was, in its essentials if not in every detail, the same as it
was in the Greek homeland: the suppliant, cleansed through a
ritual purification which included fasting (and, it may be,
sexual abstinence as well), would bed down for the night in
the sanctuary and pray to the god to send a dream revealing
the cure. The suppliant invalid was by now at a peak of
mystical emotion, a peak of self-induced receptivity to
nocturnal visions. But even so the god might fail to oblige, and
for suppliants anxious to guard against that eventuality there
were, near by, purveyors of arcana from whom one could
purchase instructions for a hypnagogic reverie or magical
incantation 'guaranteed' to educe the longed-for dream.

To us as we read about it, the locale and its atmosphere
resemble those of a fairground rather than of a holy place. The
avenue leading to the temple was lined with shops and booths
offering food, souvenirs, and other goods as well as services to
the visitors, a veritable captive audience of invalids and the
accompanying members of their families. Those lucrative
commercial locations lining the approach to the sanctuary
were, of course, rented out by the temple, providing one of its
many sources of steady income. Another source was the fees
that the suppliants eagerly paid: at the very least an entrance
fee, a fee for the ritual purification, and a fee for permission to
spend the night in the presence of the god. For all the visitors
there were, in addition, the not inconsiderable expenses of
travel. In sum, the opportunity to appeal to Asklepios-
Imhotep did not come cheaply. And if all went well and the
deity deigned to vouchsafe a dream, he was likely to do so
using allegorical or symbolic figures and actions. A further
expense would then be incurred, namely a fee paid to an

'expert' who would expound in layman's terms the 'true meaning' of the dream and its message. These professional dream-interpreters enjoyed a flourishing practice at shrines such as this. At Memphis the excavators found a sign which obviously once hung over the doorway of one of the booths or stalls near the temple. The sign reads: 'Cretan dream-interpreter here'. The reference to Crete was a nice touch, replete with implications and overtones: Ptolemaic Egypt had a sizeable body of immigrants from Crete (see Chapter 6); in addition, Crete was famed throughout the world as the earliest home of Greek civilization; on both scores, then, the sign subtly promised the families of the Greek-speaking élite of Egypt information based upon the 'genuine and original tradition of the homeland', a tradition expressing the experience of centuries, none of your new, strange, and untried lore from upstart practitioners.

At shrines elsewhere in Egypt, Serapis himself dispensed therapeutic dreams. At Memphis, however, while dominating the whole temple complex Serapis does not appear to have impinged directly upon the healing function of Asklepios-Imhotep. The following account, on a papyrus found at Oxyrhynchos, appears to relate to the Memphis shrine; Imouthes in this account is the Hellenized form of the name Imhotep.

After my mother had been seized by an ungodly quartan ague and plagued by it for three years, we finally came to our senses and presented ourselves as suppliants before the god entreating him to vouchsafe a cure from the disease. And the god, ever propitious to all, appeared in dreams and cured her with simple remedies, and we rendered the due sacrifices of gratitude to our saviour. Not long after, when I was suddenly seized with a pain in my right side, I rushed to the helper of the human race and he again readily heeded the call of pity and displayed even more effectively his particular beneficence, which I will confirm as I recount his awesome powers.

It was night, when every living creature was asleep except those in pain, and divine influence could manifest itself more effectively. I was burning with a high fever and convulsed with panting and coughing caused by the pain emanating from my side. Heavy in the head and drowsy from the pain, I was dropping off into sleep, but my mother—as mothers do with children, being naturally devoted—suffered at my tortures and sat by my side without sleeping a wink.

Then suddenly she saw—it was no dream and she was not even sleeping, for her eyes were wide open, though not sharply focused—there came to her a divine apparition, which so startled her that it easily prevented her from observing either the god or his servants closely. Anyway, there was a figure, taller than human, clad in shining raiment carrying a book in his left hand; it only looked at me from head to foot two or three times and disappeared. My mother, after recovering herself, tried, still trembling, to wake me. She found me sweating profusely but free of the fever, made obeisance to the epiphany of the god, then wiped me and calmed me. Then we spoke, and she started to tell me about the god's potency but I anticipated her and gave her a complete account myself; for everything she had seen in the vision had appeared to me in dreams. After relieving these pains in my side the god gave me yet another assuaging cure and I proclaimed his benefactions. But when we again besought his favour with sacrifices according to our ability, he on his part, through the priest who attends him in holy rituals, demanded the fulfilment of the promise long since announced to him. We therefore, though knowing that we were delinquent neither in sacrifices nor in votive offerings, nevertheless kept supplicating him again and again with these. But as he said repeatedly that his pleasure lay not there but in what had been promised, I remained perplexed until finally the divine obligation to write this book, though I am unequal to it, occurred to me. Since, O master, you had decided that I was neglecting the divine book, invoking your superintendence and filled with your divine spirit I have hastened to the divinely imposed task. I think I can be brief and clear in spreading the word of your purpose since I have, in a treatise on nature in another book, given a simple, true, and convincing account of the creation of the universe. In writing the present book I have throughout filled in the missing and deleted the superfluous and, though engaged in a rather lengthy narrative, I have spoken succinctly and told a complicated story in straightforward fashion. Wherefore, O master, I deduce that this book has been completed in accordance with your graciousness and not my wisdom. Such writing accords with your divinity, and you are identified in the thanks of all, O greatest of gods and teacher, Asklepios, as discoverer of this art. For all votive offerings and gifts of sacrifices endure for only the immediate occasion and presently pass away, but the written word is a deathless expression of gratitude that rejuvenates the remembrance on every occasion. Every Greek tongue will tell your story and every Greek man will worship the son of Ptah, Imouthes. Assemble hither, good and kindly men, away malicious and impious! Assemble, all who have served the god and been cured of diseases, all who practise the healing art, all who will labour as zealous votaries of virtue, all who have been exalted with great abundance of good things, all who have been rescued from dangers at sea. For every place has been visited by the saving power of the god.[4]

The Children of Glaukias

A certain Glaukias, who died in 164 BC, was a cleruch of Macedonian ancestry. He was settled on land in the village of Psichis, in the Herakleopolite nome (which was just south of Memphis, and bordered the Arsinoite nome on the south and east). In the course of his military career he attained the coveted title of 'king's cousin'. His sons always remained proudly conscious of their Macedonian origins. One of them in particular, when living in the precinct of the Serapeion, surrounded by Egyptians, rarely failed in official and semi-official documents to identify himself as a 'Macedonian', or 'Macedonian by descendance'.

Glaukias had four sons and perhaps a daughter. Of the sons, Ptolemaios and Apollonios, the eldest and the youngest, eventually left home for other careers, while their two brothers, Hippalos and Sarapiōn, continued to live at Psichis. Even after their separation the four brothers remained in close contact, both personally and in matters of business. A Berenikē mentioned in the archive may have been their sister; an alternative interpretation of the slight evidence relating to her sees her as Sarapion's wife.

Ptolemaios, the eldest son, was born toward the end of the third century BC. As the son of an officer of Macedonian origins, he would have received the rudiments of a Greek education in his native village. A reference in one of the documents points to the possibility—but it is no more than that—that he once visited Alexandria; and if he did it was not, as with the scions of many Greek and Macedonian families, to further his formal education, but only to transact a piece of business. We see from the papyri of the archive that he could write but never learned to do so with ease or great skill; moreover, his spelling was purely phonetic, his grammar shaky at best. In the year 172 BC, when he was thirty or so, he entered voluntarily into seclusion from the outside world, taking up residence in the small temple of Astartē that stood within the close of The Great Serapeion, being received there by the god Serapis as a 'confined person', that is a recluse 'in the service of the god'. The extant papyri give us no statement of the reason or reasons that led Ptolemaios to make so radical a change in his lifestyle. Perhaps he was undergoing a climacteric—the 'identity crisis' of approaching middle age, in today's expression. Alternatively or additionally, since the documents do reveal that he was given to dreaming dreams of elaborate and highly charged emotional content (we shall look at those dreams later in this chapter), it is possible to imagine that he took up residence in the sanctuary in response to a divine command that he received, or thought he received, in one of his dreams. ('A dream too comes from Zeus,' was an age-old Greek notion, as we learn from Homer's putting those words into Achilles' mouth in the *Iliad*.)[5] But these are, of course, mere conjectures; if Ptolemaios ever recorded why he entered upon the life of a recluse, that record has perished.

Ptolemaios lived in the close of the Serapeion for twenty years or more, presumably until his death. His duties 'in the service of the god' are never detailed in any of the documents of the archive. Obviously there was no need for such an account, as he and his contemporaries knew perfectly well what was involved. We today are able to deduce, in a general way, that such recluses were popularly believed to enjoy the special favour of their patron god, who employed them as (among other things) mouthpieces for oracles and prophecies. The archive is silent on whether Ptolemaios himself performed any such function. One thing we do learn about the conditions of his existence is that, while the reclusive life did restrict his movements to the confines of the Serapeion precinct, he could obtain release from his 'bondage' on very special occasions, such as that of his brother Sarapion's wedding. Nor was he required to abandon all secular activities, or to sever all ties with the outside world. He communicated freely with his brothers and with government officers on the outside; the latter, as representatives of the royal power, exercised an overriding authority over the internal autonomy of the sanctuary. Although the temple paid Ptolemaios a monthly stipend—a stipend often delayed, as papers in the archive record—of 100 drachmas and a ration of grain and oil, he relied upon his brothers to supply him with some of the basic necessities of life, bread and other foodstuffs. With that fraternal assistance (no doubt his share of the produce from their paternal estate) supplementing his temple stipend, his financial situation appears to have been a comfortable, if not an opulent, one.

Ptolemaios, as the eldest son, had a very special tie to the youngest, Apollonios, who was no more than eight or nine years old when their father died. From then on the nearly middle-aged Ptolemaios, from his residence in the Serapeion, served the boy *in loco parentis*. When food was brought to Ptolemaios from Psichis, it was usually Apollonios who brought it. Then too, Ptolemaios came quickly to rely upon the writing skill that the boy demonstrated from a very early age, and nearly half the documents in the archive are in Apollonios' easily recognizable handwriting. But Apollonios' sole virtue as a scribe was his ability to write fast; for the rest, his writing is uneven and unattractive in appearance, his spelling even worse than his older brother's, and his grammar rudimentary and erratic.

Still, the boy was willing, persistent and (as will soon appear) indefatigable when necessary. Even before he came of age, Ptolemaios had already given him what amounted to a power of attorney to be exercised in transactions taking place outside the sanctuary. A little later, when he was fifteen or sixteen, Apollonios lived as a recluse in the same Astartē temple of the Serapeion as his brother Ptolemaios, but that experiment was given up after a few months. As we shall presently see in some detail, Ptolemaios had learnt in fourteen years to cope, more or less, with the anti-Greek attitudes and actions of the preponderantly Egyptian personnel of the sanctuary, but when the hostility and violence engulfed Apollonios as well, Ptolemaios decided against exposing his younger brother to a lifetime of such unpleasantness and danger, and he acted with exemplary promptitude to find a more secure niche for the boy. On learning that the king and queen were soon to visit Memphis and its shrines, he prepared two petitions. In one he complained—for at least, to our knowledge, the third time in seven years—of physical violence done to him by Egyptians, including priests and acolytes. In the other he asked the king to enrol Apollonios, an officer's son, in the Graeco-Macedonian military corps stationed at Memphis, a step which, in addition to giving Apollonios a settled career, would have the further advantages of adding a soldier's pay to the family finances, and of providing Ptolemaios with a well-connected champion on the outside to bring him official support in his frequent clashes with Egyptians inside the sanctuary. Fortunately for us, one of the documents in the archive contains the record that Apollonios kept, in his own handwriting, of the petition and its sequel:

Year 24, Thoth 2 [3 October 158 BC], I presented the petition to the king and queen.

To King Ptolemy and Queen Kleopatra his sister, gods *philometores* ['mother-loving'], greeting from Ptolemaios son of Glaukias, Macedonian by descendance, from the Herakleopolite nome. My aforementioned father Glaukias, one of the 'king's cousin' colonists in the Herakleopolite nome, lost his life in the time of the troubles.[6] Among his survivors are myself and my younger brother Apollonios. But as it happens that I have been a recluse in The Great Serapeion at Memphis for fifteen years, and as I have no children [to support me], I am obliged to secure for my aforesaid brother a military appointment, whereby I, continuing in my condition of recluse, will be able to have his assistance and live decently. I therefore beg you, greatest gods *philometores*, to take into consideration the above-mentioned [fifteen] years and—inasmuch as I have no source of the necessities of life other than, by fleeing for refuge to you, greatest gods and helpers, to obtain the indicated military appointment for my brother—if it please you, to give me too a share in the succour that you afford to all such religious servants, by ordering that instructions be sent to the appropriate officers to enrol my above-mentioned brother Apollonios under the banner of Dexilaos, which [unit] is garrisoned at Memphis, and to issue to him the same pay and rations as those men receive, so that I may live decently and be able to offer sacrifices for you and your children, [praying] that you may be for all time lords of every land that Helios shines upon. When that is done, I shall have received through you my subsistence for life. Farewell.

[King's order] Let it be done, and let the record show how much it will cost.

[Also from the king] To Demetrios: [See that] Apollonios, a Macedonian, is enrolled under the banner of Dexilaos, which [unit] is garrisoned at Memphis, and that he is duly issued all that the others receive, viz. 150 drachmas and three artabs of wheat, one artab of the wheat in kind and in lieu of the other two 100 drachmas. [Date, 4 February 157.]

There follows (omitted here for the sake of concision) a memorandum by Demetrios summarizing the above documents for the commander of the Memphis garrison, with copies to three other high officials. Apollonios then concludes with his own summary.

[In October 158] I delivered the petition to the king and queen, and I received it back from him [*sic*] and delivered it sealed to Demetrios, and I received it back from him and brought it to Aristōn and to Dioskouridēs, the secretary in the accountant's office, and from Dioskourides to Chairemōn and from Chairemon to Apollodoros and he presented it at court on [25 January 157], and I received the two royal orders issued in response to that presentation, one addressed to Demetrios and one to Dioskourides, and from Demetrios, 'chief bodyguard' and chief of commissariat, I received four letters, one to Posidonios, nome strategos, one to Ammonios, paymaster-in-chief, one to Kallistratos, secretary, and one to Dioskourides, 'king's friend' and finance minister. The orders and letters were delivered and given to be read to the finance minister, and I received the order back from Ptolemaios his secretary and the letter from Epimenēs [head of his correspondence bureau] and brought them to Isidoros the independent auditor[?], and from him I brought them to Philoxenos, and from him I brought them to Artemon and from him to Lykos, and he made a copy [of each], and I brought them to the correspondence bureau to Sarapion and from him to Eubios and from him to Doriōn, and he made a copy, and back again to Sarapion and they were [again] submitted to the finance minister to be read, and I received them from Epimenes and brought them to Sarapion and he wrote to Nikanōr and he wrote two letters, one to Dorion the treasury officer and one to Posidonios the strategos of the Memphite nome.[7]

The present-day reader, however hardened by the indifferent and exasperating ways of modern bureaucracy, cannot but be struck by the number of papers and signatures Apollonios had to collect and the number of officials he had to call upon between the time the petition was first submitted and the time the appointment was finally authorized and effected. But the picture is not altogether so depressing as it appears at first glance. It is clear that Apollonios' appointment had to be acted upon and recorded by not one but two important branches of government, the financial administration (for the payment of the stipend) as well as the military. Then again, the fact that the matter came twice before the finance minister must presumably be seen not as duplication of effort or as just 'more paper work', but as indicating that somewhere along the line an error of omission or commission was found. The papers were then put through again with the necessary corrections, and after all his running around from office to office Apollonios finally obtained what he wanted. And clearly he regarded the appointment, with its status, emoluments, and perquisites, as being well worth all the effort involved in getting it.

In the ensuing years we often find Apollonios making trips home to Psichis, bringing food supplies from there to Ptolemaios, or simply visiting his brother at the sanctuary. Such 'compassionate' leaves were doubtless one of the perquisites of his military status. There are a few documents in the archive which suggest, if we read between the lines, that Apollonios managed such frequent visits to his recluse brother by getting himself assigned to advise and assist the police post of the temple in its task of apprehending criminals and disturbers of the peace. But before we go further into that police matter, our attention is claimed by the twins, Thauēs and Taous.

The Twins

It was an age-old Egyptian ritual at Memphis that when a sacred Apis bull died, a pair of female twins was appointed to symbolize Isis and Nephthys in observing the seventy-day period of mourning. Those twins were then retained and maintained in the Serapeion as cult attendants of the new Apis bull until it died, whereupon a new pair of mourning women was installed, and the cycle was repeated.

As already remarked, under the Ptolemies the Egyptian priestly establishment provided the socio-political, as well as the religious, leadership of the native Egyptian population. With the aim of obtaining the support of the powerful clergy—or, failing that, of at least tempering their opposition—the Ptolemaic rulers from the very beginning of their dynasty made a special point of publicly observing the more important of the Egyptian religious ceremonies (and much of the Graeco-Macedonian population followed their lead in this). Thus, for example, they celebrated the festivals of Isis, and they frequently attended the solemn rites of the burial of the Apis bull and the acclamation of its successor. The Ptolemies also maintained a close relationship with the family in which the Memphite high-priesthood was hereditary. And at least from the reign of Ptolemy V, each new ruler of the dynasty was crowned by the high priest of the god Ptah, in whose temple Apis was worshipped at Memphis.[8]

During seven or more years of Ptolemaios' residence in the Serapeion the twin attendants of the Apis cult were named Thaues and Taous. They appear in some fifty documents, nearly half the total of the archive. Even before their appointment in the Apis cult, Ptolemaios, an old friend of their father's, had taken them under his wing, and thereafter he remained their protector and representative in contacts and correspondence with officialdom. While literate in the Egyptian language, the twins could not write Greek. Whether they could speak Greek, or whether Ptolemaios had to communicate with them in their native tongue, we cannot say; the archive is ambiguous on that point.

The story of how the twins were driven to appeal to Ptolemaios for help is told in a petition which he and his brother Apollonios drafted for them not long after their arrival in the Serapeion. The petition is extant in three versions, a brief first one, a somewhat longer and more detailed second, and a more polished third, the final form in which the petition was actually submitted. We can get the story in its essentials from the first one, supplemented by an extract from the second. Note in particular that their Egyptian mother left her Egyptian husband to live with a Greek soldier, whose superior status undoubtedly accounts, at least in good part, for her arrogant treatment of her Egyptian daughters.

To King Ptolemy and Queen Kleopatra, his sister, gods *philometores*, greeting from Thaues and Taous, twins performing ritual service in

The Great Serapeion at Memphis, pouring libations to Osorapis for the welfare of you and your children. Being wronged on many counts by our mother Nephoris and her son Pakhratēs [our half-brother], we flee for refuge to you, that we may obtain justice. Our mother left our father and moved in with Philippos son of Sōgenēs, a soldier in ———'s unit, and she treacherously egged on Philippos to kill our father, and drawing his sword he went for him. But our father's house is near the river, so he jumped into the river and swam under water till he came to an island in the river and a boat picked him up and deposited him in Herakleopolis, where he died of grief. His brothers went and got him, brought him back and delivered him to the cemetery, where he lies still unburied [i.e., Nephoris has not performed the prescribed ritual]. But she took possession of his property and collects a monthly rent of 1,400 copper drachmas. She threw us out [of our house] and, starving, we fled up to the Serapeion, to Ptolemaios, one of the recluses there. Ptolemaios, who was a friend of our father's, received us and feeds us. When the mourning [for Apis] occurred, [the priests] took us down [to the crypt] to lament for the god. Acquaintances of Nephoris persuaded us to take on her son Pakhrates to assist us . . . and in return he stole whatever we had in the Serapeion and what he had brought us from the royal commissary, viz., a metretes of oil, and went back to his mother. But Ptolemaios, who is a recluse in the said sanctuary, at the god's behest received us. . . .

The first draft of the petition ends here and was never completed. The second draft ended with the formulaic request, seen repeatedly in Chapter 4, to have the nome strategos instruct the local officials to recover the stolen property and 'compel her, if she holds any of our paternal estate illegally, to give it back, so that we may be succoured by you'.[9]

Most of the other documents in which the twins figure are requests for, or accounts of, oil and other rations. Standing out in sharp contrast to those pedestrian affairs are the dreams that are recorded in three Greek papyri and two Demotic texts (one on papyrus, one on an ostracon). In one instance one of the twins is the dreamer, but mostly they act or speak in dreams dreamt by Ptolemaios.[10]

1. The dream that the girl Thaues, one of a twin, saw on Pachon 17th: I seemed in my dream to be walking down the street, counting nine houses. I wanted to turn back. I said, 'All this is at most nine.'

They say, 'Well, you are free to go.' I said, 'It is too late for me.'

2. The dream that Ptolemaios saw at the Moon Festival on Pachon 25th: I seem to see Thaues singing aloud in a rather sweet voice and in good spirits; and I see Taous laughing, and her foot is big and clean.

3. On the 29th: Two men are working in the vestibule. Taous is sitting on the steps and joking with them, and on hearing the voice of Khentosney she immediately turns black. They said that they would teach her . . . [The rest is lost.]

4. Dream of Ptolemaios, Pachon 15th: Two men came to me and said to me, 'Ptolemaios, take the copper coins for the blood.' They count out a hundred copper drachmas for me, and for Thaues, the twin-girl, a purse full of copper four-drachma pieces. They say to her, 'See, the copper coins for the blood.' I said to them, 'She has more coppers than I.'

5. The dream that I saw on Pachon 20th: I seemed to be counting [the days of the month], saying, 'Year 20 Thoth 1st, [2nd, etc.], up to the 20th.'

6. Year 23 Pachon 4th: I seemed in my dream to be calling repeatedly upon the very great god Ammon to come to me from the north in his trinity. At last he arrives. It seems to me there is a cow in the place and she is heavy with young. He takes hold of the cow and lays her on the ground. He inserts his hand into her swollen belly and draws out a bull.

7. What I saw in my sleep—may it bring me luck! Pachon 23rd, my birthday.

Ptolemaios to Damoxenos, greeting. Year 23 in the night of Tybi 12th to 13th. I seemed [in a dream] to be walking in Memphis from west to east, and I come upon a pile of chaff and a man coming to me from the west also comes upon it and as for me—my eyes were sort of closed and suddenly I open my eyes and what do I see but the twin girls in the schoolroom of Tothēs. They called.

I said, 'See that you be not faint-hearted. Tothes has wearied of finding the way to me because I have reversed my bed.'

I heard Tothes say, 'Get away. Why do you say that? I will bring the twins to you.'

I see you yourself bringing them, and I advance to meet them until I reach them, and I walk in the street with them. I said to them, 'I have but a brief time left in this upper air, and what I was will disappear tomorrow morning.'

At once I saw one of them go to a dark place in someone's house, and she sits down and makes water. I saw at once that the other of them had been sitting off to one side. I told Harmaïs to let[?] him come.

I also saw much more, and I again implored Sarapis and Isis, saying, 'Come to me, goddess of goddesses, be gracious and hear me: Pity the twins, you destined them to be twins. Release me, for see! I am a greybeard and I know that I shall come to an end in a short time. But they will be women, and if they are defiled they will never become clean.'

On the 14th I seemed [in a dream] to be on a big tower in Alexandria. I had a handsome face and I didn't want to show my face to anyone because it was so beautiful. An old woman sat down by my side and a crowd gathered to north and east of me. They shout that a man had been burned to a crisp, and the old woman says to me, 'Wait a minute and I will lead you to the god Knephis, so you can kneel and worship him.'

And I seemed to be saying to an old man, 'Father, do you not see this vision that I have beheld?' I told him in detail. He gave me two reeds. I looked through them and soon saw Knephis. Rejoice, all my friends, I shall soon have my release. I have beheld other visions, but these are altogether more beautiful. You know that my chief concern is to assure a safe harbour for the twins. I worry about nothing else. So then, invite the twins to come to you and say that I am leaving. Amosis has come to me and has granted me free passage and I am leaving my cell.

The first [dream]: I am walking in the portico of Serapis with a woman named Tawē, who is a virgin. I ask her, 'Tawe, is your heart perplexed?' She answers, 'My sister Taous will be angry with me.'

The second: I hear someone say to a man, 'Call out, "Apollonios, you are a Greek, —— is an Egyptian." '

The third: I am in my house with my older brother, who is crying.

The fourth: I find a man who belongs to those illegally in the place.

The fifth: . . . woman . . . [The rest is lost.]

The first [dream]: The dreaming girl dreams she is in Memphis. She is told that her mother is threatened by the rising flood of the Nile. She swims over and rescues her in the temple of Anubis. . . .

Another: I am in the house . . . Someone says that Horos, the scribe, is taking the girl, my sister, to wife. I must talk with her, to ask if he loves her. I say to him, 'Love her, my sister.' If he loves her she will love him . . . [The rest is lost.]

Year 22 Pharmouthi 5th. The dreams that Nektembēs saw involving the twins and myself:

The first dream. I saw Apollonios coming towards me. He says, 'A good greeting to you, Nektembes.'

The second. *Phaphere si enreëx* in Boubastos *khmenni* in the house of Ammon *pel lel khason khani.*

The third. I saw Ptolemaios with a knife in his hand, walking in the street. He knocks at a door and it is opened. He tussles, trying to strike him. I say, 'Don't do it or you will destroy your slave. A master doesn't destroy his own slave.'

The fourth. A woman is seated on a mat, one child on the mat with her and another on another mat facing her. I say to her, 'Your mat is producing vegetables and cabbage.' She remained seated and didn't move.

Pharmouthi 24th. The dreams that Nektembes saw about the divine custody of the twins and myself, that I have had bad luck with my house:

[The first dream.] A man seemed to be saying to me, 'Bring me the leather [sandal] of your foot and I will give you the leather of my foot.' I say, 'I don't want to.'

The second. It seemed to me someone was cleaning a house, sweeping it clean.

The third. A dove seemed to fly out of my hand, and I run after it, saying, 'I am certainly not going to let it escape.' I catch it and put it in my left hand, and I confined it with a palm frond, to keep it from escaping.

The fourth. It seemed to me two women were sitting with a man. They joke with him and swear thus: 'By holy Isis.'

[List of dreams.]
    About my brother.
    About Ptolemaios.
    About Thaues.
    About Sarapion, where he will be.
    In the dream about Thaues—Harpaēsis, and the words 'Ptolemaios to a crisp'.

' . . . even though I am a Greek'

A god with attributes of both Hellenic and Egyptian divinity, Serapis was, as already remarked, very popular with the people of both those cultures. Both also readily accepted the syncretisms of their other gods, Isis with Demeter, Imhotep with Asklepios, Hathor with Aphrodite, and so on (different

localities, in fact, sometimes preferred different identifications).
But this easy acceptance of the gods themselves did not always
imbue the relationships among their votaries. In The Great
Serapeion at Memphis the temple personnel, lay and priestly,
was (we gather) predominantly Egyptian. The happy relationship between the Egyptian twin girls and their benefactor,
Ptolemaios of Macedonian descent, even though that relationship stemmed from rather unusual circumstances, may well
reflect the general tenor of the day-to-day existence in the
temple precinct. But even if mutual tolerance and comity were
the norm, many of the Egyptians nursed feelings of resentment at the presence and position of individuals such as
Ptolemaios, members of the Greek-speaking ruling class,
whom they regarded as interlopers in their sacred preserve.
That hostility was never eradicated, or even attenuated with
the passage of time. On the contrary, it intensified with time,
being but a locally focused, locally aggravated aspect of the
pervasive Egyptian resentment of Greek privilege, a resentment that simmered not far below the surface of daily life; as
we have already seen in Chapters 1 and 4, even a slight
provocation might cause this resentment to erupt in spiteful
and violent actions. In the Serapeion one such incident
occurred, we know, in 163 BC. Here is Ptolemaios' account of
it.

To Dionysios, 'king's friend' and strategos, from Ptolemaios son of
Glaukias, Macedonian, a recluse in The Great Serapeion these ten
years. I am wronged by those who take turns serving as bakers in the
said temple. . . . On [12 November] they appeared at the little
Astartē shrine in which I live in divine service, and forced their way
in with the intention of dragging me out and driving me away, just
as they tried to do also in earlier years, when the revolt was on—and
that despite the fact that I am a Greek! When I realized that they
had taken leave of their senses, I locked myself in, but they found my
associate, Harmaïs, in the entranceway and beat him with their
bronze tools. I therefore ask you to order that instructions be sent to
Menedēmos, the chief of your police post in the Anubis shrine here,
to force them to give me my rights, and if they do not abide [by his
order] to send them to you, so that you, who hate wickedness, may
render judgement about them. Farewell.
[From the strategos] To Menedemos: See that he obtains his rights.

As Ptolemaios says, that was not the first such attack, nor was it to be the last. Another, just two years later, elicited the following petition:

To Dionysios, 'king's friend' and strategos, from Ptolemaios son of Glaukias, Macedonian, a recluse in The Great Serapeion these twelve years. As I have been outrageously wronged and repeatedly placed at risk of life by the temple cleaners named below, I [hereby] flee to you for succour, thinking thus to obtain my rights. On [9 November 161] they appeared in the Astartē shrine within the temple precinct, in which I happen to have lived the aforesaid years as a recluse in divine service, and they tried, some with stones in their hands, others with rods, to force their way in, in order to plunder the temple on some pretext and to kill me—and that despite the fact that I am a Greek! . . . I beat them to the door and locked it, and at the top of my voice exhorted them to withdraw in peace, but even then they did not depart, and when a certain Diphilos, one of the neighbouring votaries in the service of Sarapis, expressed his indignation at how they were carrying on in such a holy place, they shoved him and maltreated and beat him outrageously, so that their lawless violence was plain for all to see. Those same persons treated me similarly in [November of 163], and I petitioned you at that very time, but I had no one to make them abide by [your ruling on] that petition, with the result that they remained unreproved, and they advanced to even greater contempt. I therefore ask you, if you see fit, to order them to be haled before you, so that they may suffer the appropriate punishment. Farewell.
[The accused are] Mys, the clothing seller, Psosnaus, porter, Imouthēs, baker, Harembasnis, grain seller, Stotoētis, porter, and with them others whose names I do not know.

There apparently was another such incident some three years after this one, and still another attack less than two years after that, on which occasion Ptolemaios addressed his complaint to the king and queen, telling them that 'the personnel of the temple are wicked and they besiege me despite the fact that I am a Greek . . . I was beset by a mob of them, who stoned me through my window.' That is the last attack of which we have a record in the extant archive, but there is no reason to suppose that they did not continue on and off so long as Ptolemaios remained resident in the Serapeion.[11]

We have come to the middle of the second century BC, and have just witnessed a situation in which some part, at least, of the Egyptian element in the population is much less cowed and quiescent, much more aggressive, than we saw in the preceding century. This historical watershed was not an accidental phenomenon, nor was it an isolated one peculiar to the Serapeion at Memphis. This was also a time, as we have seen and shall see again, when the royal sway, under an ever-present threat from outside powers and the debilitating effects of repeated dynastic wars within, had begun an irreversible decline from the unassailable sovereignty of the first century of Ptolemaic rule. The interrelation of these developments is fairly obvious. As we proceed in the following chapters through the latter half of the second into the first century, we shall observe an increasing assertiveness of Egyptian ways and values, especially, but not exclusively, in localities lacking a strong Greek-descended presence.

6

A Greek Stationed among Egyptians: Cavalry Officer Dryton and his Family

Time: The directly related documents were written *c.*150–99 BC, but they include references to events as far back as the year 176/5. One document of 174 BC has been thought by some to belong to this archive, and one of 162 BC records a purchase of land by a man from whom the property was acquired two years later by an aunt of Dryton's wife Apollonia.

Place: In the Thebaid, in the area from Ptolemais to Pathyris (Map 3).

Documents: Some forty in all, including five Greek ostraca and a dozen Demotic papyri. Half the Greek papyri are in London, and the rest of the documents are scattered among collections in Berlin, Cairo, Chicago, Fribourg, Giessen, Heidelberg, Mainz, Manchester, New York, Paris, and Strasbourg. There are probably others still unpublished; the Demotic papyrus in Chicago, for example, though purchased in 1920, was not unrolled until 1979 and not published until 1984.

Family tree: See Figs. 1 and 2.

Drytōn son of Pamphilos was born *c.*195 BC, a citizen of Ptolemais, the Greek city in Upper Egypt. He had one, possibly two, brothers, whether younger or older than himself we cannot say. He died between 113 and 111 BC, which made his an unusually long life for those times—more than twice the average life expectancy. A man described in a papyrus of 174 BC as having long hair worn brushed up and being long-faced and hook-nosed, is thought by some scholars to have been Dryton, but the identification must be regarded as dubious since that man is described as light-skinned. In the will that

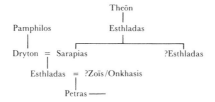

Fig. 1. Family tree of Dryton: earlier marriage

Dryton drew up when he was close to fifty years old his appearance is given as 'of medium height, dark-skinned . . . with a scar on his right eyebrow, and bald'. From long-haired youth to middle-aged baldpate is a common enough transition, but not a change of skin colour.[1]

Dryton spent his entire adult life as a soldier in garrison and police duty at posts just north and south of Great Diospolis ('City of Zeus'), as Thebes was renamed under the Ptolemies. The documents of the archive reveal that he could read and write, but nothing more about the level of his education. He belonged to the *politeuma* of Cretans, to which he could have been assigned merely as a matter of administrative convenience (p. 31). However, both his own name and that of his son (named after his maternal grandfather) point to the Dorian area of the Greek world, to which Crete belonged, as the original home of both families, Dryton's and that of his wife, Sarapias'. Just when those families migrated to Egypt is not revealed by the documents of the archive—they could have been among the settlers of Ptolemais at its creation, or they could have come at any time in the intervening hundred years—but the story of Dryton's life, as it unfolds in this chapter, sounds like that of a man whose family had lived in Egypt for more than a single generation.

Sarapias was, like Dryton, a citizen of Ptolemais. Whether she was his first or his second wife is something of a puzzle. There is a reference in one of the documents to a will that Dryton prepared back in 176/5 BC. As we know that Dryton drew up another will (it survives in two fragmentary copies) about the time of his later marriage, it has generally been supposed that the earlier will was occasioned by this first

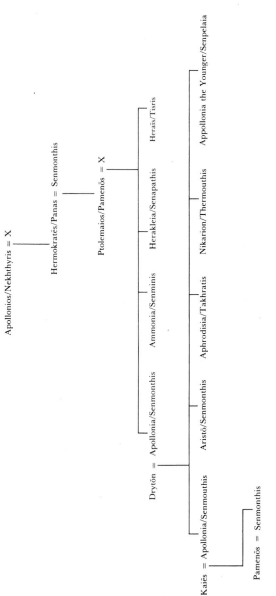

The sign / separates a Greek name (left) from the same person's Egyptian name (right) as it is spelled in Greek documents. Hellenization of the Egyptian names usually involved, at a minimum, providing them with a Greek declensional ending, plus a certain amount of variation in the vocalization: e.g. Nekhthyris of the Greek documents appears in the Demotic as Nakhthor, Pa- and Tamenōs in Greek represent Pa- and Tamenhō, etc.

Fig. 2. Later marriage (immediate family only)

marriage, and that that marriage was to Sarapias. Dryton
would have been about eighteen or twenty years old then, a
suitable age for a bridegroom in his first marriage; and indeed
it is hard to imagine why else such a young man would want
to have a testamentary instrument prepared and recorded.
The difficulty of interpretation arises from the fact that the
only child of Sarapias ever mentioned in the archive is a son,
Esthladas, born *c.*158 BC. Therefore, if Dryton married
Sarapias in 176 BC, we must adopt one of two suppositions,
neither of them really satisfactory: either Sarapias was barren
for the first fifteen years and more of their married life (in
which case Dryton might well have divorced her long before
Esthladas was born); or else she experienced during those
years a succession of miscarriages, or still births, or live births
followed by the death of each such infant at an early age. That
none of such a succession of children should have survived
prior to Esthladas (whom she would have borne when she was
well past thirty) is statistically highly unlikely. On the other
hand, if Esthladas was in the normal course of events born
soon after his mother's marriage to Dryton, that marriage is
not likely to have been the first for Dryton, who was by then
approaching the age of forty. First wife or second, Sarapias
disappears from the archive soon after the birth of Esthladas.
Her marriage to Dryton may have ended in divorce, but it
seems on the whole likelier that she died. At any rate, before
he was ten years old her son had a stepmother and a new place
of abode, Pathyris.[2]

The circumstances of Dryton's transfer to Pathyris were the
following. In the first half of the second century BC the
Egyptian throne had been rocked by invasion from Syria and
by native uprisings within the country. The traditional centre
of such disaffection and resistance was Thebes, the stronghold
of the wealthy, prestigious, and powerful priests of the
Egyptian sun-god. In addition, since 167 BC the king, Ptolemy
VI, and his younger brother (who outlived and later
succeeded him, to enjoy the longest reign of the dynasty) had
been at daggers' point in their battle for the throne, and a
throne seen to be shaky might easily invite fresh outbreaks of
rebellion. Finally, in planning the counterblow invasion of
Syria which he launched a few years later, Ptolemy VI would

doubtless, as an elementary precaution, have increased the guard around the principal centres of potential trouble. Some or all of the above were among the considerations that impelled the king to establish (or strengthen) garrisons at Pathyris and nearby Krokodilopolis, thus isolating Thebes in the military pincers between those posts to its south and those at Ptolemais and Little Diospolis to its north.

Dryton was transferred to Pathyris *c.*152 BC, remarried there soon after, and was domiciled there for the rest of his life. One or more tours of duty at Krokodilopolis did not really break the even tenor of his existence at Pathyris, as the two posts were within easy reach of each other—near enough, so one document tells us, for the two places to share a priest. On at least one occasion, *c.*136 BC, Dryton was transferred back to garrison duty at Little Diospolis, but the transfer to a post a day's journey (some seventy kilometres) from home was presumably of a temporary nature.

The remove to Pathyris marked not simply a geographical change, but also a cultural one, a veritable climacteric in Dryton's life. From the Hellenic milieu of Ptolemais and Little Diospolis, the milieu in which he was born and spent the first half of his life, he and the other men of his cavalry unit moved into a town inhabited almost entirely by Egyptians. The people of Pathyris conducted their daily affairs in their native language; in fact, as we shall observe presently, very few of them had mastered, or found it necessary to master, Greek to any usable extent. Accordingly, from the time he was posted to Pathyris, Dryton's lifestyle became less and less Greek, more and more Egyptian. The first sign of that evolution comes to us in the marriage that he contracted a year or two after arriving in Pathyris. A glance at the family tree shows that Dryton and his former wife Sarapias came from families in which all the names were Greek, while the members of his new wife's family all bore Egyptian as well as Greek names. It is thus no surprise to find some of the later documents in the Dryton archive written in Demotic, as the then current Egyptian cursive script is called today.[3]

The wife that Dryton took in Pathyris was a teenaged girl some twenty-five or even thirty years younger than himself. She was one, probably the eldest, of four sisters in a local military family enrolled in the *politeuma* of Cyrenaeans. That could mean that one of her forebears had been among the many recruits known to have been attracted to Ptolemaic Egypt in the third century BC from the North African city of Cyrene, a Greek colony, but the greater likelihood is that hers was an Egyptian family in origin which had acquired a Greek veneer through intermarriage. Her father, known by the Greek name of Ptolemaios and the Egyptian name of Pamenōs, was, like his father and his father's brother before him, a foot-soldier stationed at Pathyris. He and Dryton met when the latter's cavalry unit was transferred to Pathyris and placed under the same general command. For the Graeco-Egyptian bride, and by extension for her parents and sisters as well, the union with Dryton was a coup, a big step up socially: her husband was not in the infantry (to which almost all Egyptian soldiers were relegated) but in the élite cavalry; moreover, he was not just *in* the cavalry but was a cavalry officer; and even more important than all that, his ancestry was pure Greek, not Graeco-Egyptian. We shall never know with what emotions Apollonia/Senmonthis accepted this husband old enough to be her father, but he was undoubtedly a rare catch in that overwhelmingly Egyptian town, and any chagrin she may have felt at his age was doubtless soothed by the enhanced social and economic position she enjoyed as his wife. In fact, we find that she relished her new status, even flaunted it, and cleverly used it to establish herself in the years to come as a woman of substance and independent means, a woman to be reckoned with. We notice that whenever possible she dropped her Egyptian name and patronym, styling herself simply Apollonia, Cyrenaean, daughter of Ptolemaios.

To Dryton this alliance with a numerous local family brought entrée into the community in which he was henceforth to live. More specifically, it brought him a handsome dowry, along with a wife who quickly demonstrated the skills of a shrewd manager of his household and was, as she soon proved, reproductively prolific. Over a period of close to twenty years she bore him five daughters, the last two of whom may have been twins. (Whether they also produced other children who did not survive, we do not know.) Apollonia/Senmouthis was the eldest daughter; the other girls are shown to the right of her in the family tree in their probable order of birth. As was customary in their mother's family, each child was given a Greek name and an Egyptian name.

Apollonia/Senmonthis, Dryton's wife, had three sisters and no brothers, five daughters and no sons. Those facts reflect another Egyptian value to which Dryton's life now conformed. Greeks throughout antiquity did not hesitate to discard unwanted neonates, exposing them to the elements to die. That fate doubtless awaited girls more often than boys, since (among other things) girls represented a future, if not immediate, financial drain—they would have to be provided with dowries. But the Egyptian religion, like the Jewish, forbade infanticide. Egyptian families kept all their children who were not snatched from them by disease, and so now did Dryton in this latter, Egyptianizing phase of his life.[4]

Besides, the children in Dryton's life were not felt as a financial burden. He had, to begin with, his soldier's stipend. In addition he was, even before moving to Pathyris, a man of property, in possession of a vineyard out in the country as well as of buildings and house lots in Great Diospolis. After the move he expanded his holdings with the acquisition of farmland in the Pathyrite region. His new wife also owned property, and her wealth too was increased by Dryton's and her own able management. Esthladas, too, by the time he was twenty, owned some property—a gift from his father, perhaps, or an inheritance from his mother—which brought him an income.[5]

The family was so well off, in fact, that it was also able to derive a substantial income from making loans in money and in kind, a favourite source of quick profit for those with ready resources (p. 17). And Apollonia, at least, was not above charging usurious rates of interest, and, when necessary, using one device or another to conceal the illegality. Here, from the year 127 BC, is a loan of money for a period of four and a half months.

[Date], in Pathyris, before Asklepiadēs, keeper of records. Apollonia, Cyrenaean, daughter of Ptolemaios—with her husband, Dryton son of Pamphilos, Cretan, [long, technical, military title recited here], as her legal representative—has lent to Solōn also known as Slēis son of

Horos, and to Harmaïs son of Horos, Persians by descendance, and to ―――― daughter of Phageris, Persian—with the aforementioned Slēis, her son, as her legal representative—in copper one talent four thousand drachmas at interest of five drachmas per hundred [per month] . . . from Phaophi to Mecheir 30 of the 44th year. The borrowers shall repay this loan to Apollonia on Mecheir 30, and if they do not repay in the stated time they shall immediately forfeit the sum increased by half, and for the excess time interest at two drachmas per hundred for each hundred. The borrowers themselves are mutual sureties for the repayment of all the aforesaid contractual obligations of the loan. Apollonia shall have the right of execution upon the borrowers, and upon each one of them as she chooses, and upon all their property, exactly as would follow from the judgement of a court. I, Areios, clerk of Asklepiades, have registered it.

The rigorous provisions relating to default or delay in repayment were standard clauses in contracts of this type. What is not clear is how Apollonia managed, in a contract prepared and recorded in the public registry, to charge interest of 5 per cent a month, two and a half times the legal maximum (which is, be it noted, the rate stipulated in the penalty clause). Perhaps the conclusion to be drawn is that the higher rate was permissible in short-term loans such as this.[6]

Dating from five years earlier than the above there is a loan by Apollonia for six months

to Apollonios son of Apollodotos, also known as Psennesis son of Harsiēsis, Persian by descendance, and his wife Heraïs daughter of Ptolemaios, also known as Tisris daughter of Paous . . . thirty-five artabs of wheat free of interest. The borrowers shall repay this loan to Apollonia [at harvest time] in the month Pachōn of the 39th year in wheat that is new, pure, unadulterated, transported to her house at their own expense . . .

There follow the standard penalty and security clauses. The characterization of the loan as interest-free is not a sign that Apollonia was a kind-hearted altruist. A recent study has shown that the expression 'free of interest' employed in loan contracts was a cruel irony, a subterfuge designed to conceal a usurious interest charge by including it in the amount stated to be the principal of the loan; but it was in reality the amount to be repaid, the amount actually loaned being considerably smaller. This tells us something about Apollonia the business woman, tight-fisted and hard-headed to the point of ruthlessness.[7]

It tells us even more if the borrower Heraïs/Tisris was Apollonia's own sister. Some question about the identification is introduced by the fact that the father's name is here given as Ptolemaios/Paous, whereas we know the sisters' father as Ptolemaios/Pamenōs. On the other hand, a loan of grain from Apollonia to her sisters Herakleia/Senapathis and Heraïs/Tisris is found in one of the Demotic papyri. In the case of the loan quoted in the preceding paragraph, a loan contract written in Greek, it is on the whole easier to suppose that the scribe miswrote the father's Egyptian name than to accept the coincidence that the borrower was another woman identical in both her names and one of her patronyms with Apollonia's younger sister.[8]

Apollonia and Dryton enjoyed a stable marriage, which lasted more than thirty-five years, until Dryton's death. Their daughters, at least some of them, were not so fortunate. To be sure, they were married in due course, one to a cavalryman, two others to other soldiers, and the remaining two girls, as they belonged to a family of means and social standing, no doubt also found husbands, whose names happen not to appear in the extant documents of the archive. But when the daughters' husbands become known to us it is not in relation to their weddings but in deeds of divorce, which are written, we note with interest, in Demotic. Takhratis (the Demotic omits her Greek name, Aphrodisia) and her husband (also identified only by his Egyptian name, Psennesis) were divorced in 123 BC, the marriage, probably her second, having lasted less than three years. The marriage of another of the daughters (in the damaged state of the papyrus we cannot tell which one) and a cavalryman with the Egyptian name of Herienoupis also ended in divorce. Apollonia/Senmouthis and her husband Kaiēs appear to have enjoyed a lasting union, but the third of the Demotic divorce agreements in the archive, a document drawn up in 99 BC, dissolved the marriage of their daughter and son-in-law. This last, the best preserved of the three, is worth quoting as an example of the

Egyptian formulation of a divorce; again, only the Egyptian names are used in identifying the parties.

[Date.] Pamenōs son of Nekhoutēs, his mother being Senthotēs, says to the woman Senmonthis the Younger, daughter of Kaiēs, her mother being Senmouthis: I have dismissed you as wife. I am separated from you in the name of the marital law. I have nothing in the world to claim of you in the name of the marital law. I am he who says to you: Take yourself a husband. From this day on I will not be able to stand in your way to any place to which you may wish to go to take yourself a husband. If I find you together with any man in the world, I will not be able to say to you: you are my wife . . . [One more clause or sentence is lost here.][9]

Dryton and his wife—and their daughters, too, at least in their early years—thought of themselves as, and prided themselves on, being Greeks. But, isolated from Hellenic contacts in Pathyris, where the population was almost entirely Egyptian, they inevitably found themselves conforming more and more to the customs of their neighbours. As the years passed, the daughters of Dryton and Apollonia tended, in their Egyptian milieu, to use only their Egyptian names. The document just quoted provides a typical example of the progressive Egyptianization of their lives; other such elements and influences will appear near the end of this chapter. But meanwhile, in concentrating on Dryton's five daughters we seem to have lost sight of his son Esthladas, the offspring of his previous marriage. What had been happening to Dryton's first-born during all these years when the girls had been growing up, marrying, and sometimes divorcing?

Not long after he came to Pathyris with his father, the boy found a stepmother installed in his new home. Happily Apollonia/Senmonthis, the new wife whom his father took, proved to be nothing like the wicked stepmother of popular stereotype. For one thing, she was not very much older than Esthladas—certainly much closer in age to him than to his father—and that may well have created a special bond between them from the start. Then again, as we saw earlier, Apollonia/Senmonthis belonged by family and cultural tradition to a society that welcomed and valued children. And in addition, a girl-bride faced with building a new life in a strange home, she apparently received with empathy and understanding the orphan boy now suddenly entrusted to her care. At all events, the indications are that Esthladas' upbringing was such as to establish close ties of affection between him and his stepmother and half-sisters. Upon coming of age he followed in his father's footsteps, embarking upon a military career. Presently he married, setting up house close to his father's on land given him by his father or stepmother. His wife is never identified as such in the surviving documents of the archive, but in all likelihood her name was Zoïs/Onkhasis. The double name tells us that she belonged to one of the local Graeco-Egyptian families, most likely one of the other families of the military men in the area. She appears only once in the archive, acting for Esthladas whilst he was away on military duty in 130 BC. Esthladas and his wife had one son who is mentioned once in the archive; if there were other children they do not appear in the extant documents. The one son who does appear is identified on that one occasion only by his Egyptian name (see Fig. 1), though he doubtless had a Greek name as well.[10]

The dynastic intrigues of the royal house caused Esthladas to see active service in 130 BC, when the hostility between Ptolemy VIII and his sister and first wife, Kleopatra II, flared into open war. Kleopatra's forces were initially successful in Lower (northern) Egypt, and after seizing Alexandria she even proclaimed herself ruler of the whole country. Esthladas' unit, like most in Upper Egypt, fought for the king. On Choiak 23 [15 January] he sent the following letter to reassure his family. He includes his stepmother in the opening salutation, but the rest of the letter is addressed in the singular to his father alone.

Esthladas to his father and mother, greeting and good health. As I tell you over and over again in my letters, keep up your spirits and take good care of yourself till things settle down. Now again [I say], please reassure yourself and our family, for the news has come that Paōs [the king's general in the Thebaid] is sailing up the river next month with sufficient forces to subdue the mobs in Hermonthis and deal with them as rebels. Look after my sisters . . . Goodbye.[11]

In the course of his long life Dryton wrote three wills, at

roughly twenty-five-year intervals. The first, drawn up in
176/5 BC, is known to us only by reference. The second and
third wills are extant, each in two copies of which one is
fragmentary. Originally there may have been other copies as
well, possibly including, as we shall see shortly, a copy written
wholly or partly in Demotic.[12]

The second will was prepared *c.*150 BC, when Dryton and
Apollonia/Senmonthis were already married but before any
children had been born to them. In that testament Dryton left
his war horse and armour to his son Esthladas, then still a
boy, and the rest of his estate, in land and movable property,
to his son and his new wife in equal half shares. Against the
possibility of his dying before Esthladas came of age, he
appointed a guardian for the boy, and made similar provision
'for any children born hereafter of me and Apollonia'. That
will was written not in Pathyris but somewhere else, probably
in nearby Krokodilopolis. It was attested, as was customary,
by six witnesses. In the damaged state of the papyrus their
names and affiliations are preserved only in small part.
Enough remains, however, to show that at least some and
probably all of the witnesses were soldiers. In Krokodilopolis,
or wherever the will was drawn up, there was obviously no
shortage of men such as these, who could make their
attestations in Greek.

Quite different was the situation in Egyptian Pathyris,
where Dryton drafted and registered his third will on 29 June
126 BC. A fragment of papyrus in London was published in
1896; another fragment from the archive, in Paris, was
published in 1926; in 1976 a Dutch scholar showed that those
two fragments formed part of the same original document,
namely a text of the third will. Taken in conjunction these
fragments of Greek text give us the names and descriptions of
five of the requisite witnesses. One was a thirty-five-year-old
priest of Aphroditē and Soukhos (the Egyptian crocodile god);
another, a fifty-year-old priest and 'chief vestryman of the
temple in Pathyris'; a third, a 'priest and chief vestryman of
the same temple'; and a fourth, a forty-year-old infantryman.
After their names and physical descriptions we find the
following statement, written in Greek: 'These four signed in
native [i.e. Demotic] script because there is not in this area

the like number of Greeks.' A fifth witness, a thirty-year-old mercenary in the cavalry, the élite military service from which Egyptians were mostly excluded, signed in Greek.[13]

The other copy of the third will, much better preserved, lacks the witnesses' attestations, a fact which indicates that it was either a first draft or—much more likely, since there are none of the changes and revisions that a draft usually shows—a copy of the original. Its text reads as follows:

[Date], in Pathyris, before Asklepiadēs, keeper of records. These are the testamentary dispositions of Dryton son of Pamphilos, Cretan . . . May it be granted me in sound health to remain in control of my estate, but if I suffer some mortal event I leave and give my possessions in land, movables, cattle and whatever I may hereafter acquire as follows: To Esthladas—my son by Sarapias daughter of Esthladas son of Theōn, citizen [of Ptolemais], with whom I then lived as my lawful wife and according to a will which I filed with Dionysios, keeper of records in the archives at Little Diospolis, in the sixth year of [Ptolemy VI] Philometor [176/5 BC] . . .—my service horse and all my armour, and of my four domestic slaves the ones named Myrsinē and —— (the remaining two females, named Eirēnē and Ampelion, going to Apollonia and her sisters, the five of them), also the vine land belonging to me in —— in the Pathyrite nome and the water wells [lined with] baked bricks located in it, and the other appurtenances as well as the waggon with its gear, and the dovecote and the other half-finished one, and a courtyard bounded as follows: south, open lots belonging to the said Esthladas, north, a vaulted room belonging to Apollonia the Younger, east, a lot belonging to Petras—— son of Esthladas, west, a lot belonging to Esthladas as far as the door opening to the west. The remaining rooms and furnishings and . . . and an open lot intended for the dovecote below Esthladas' door and west of the vaulted room I give to Apollonia and Aristo and Aphrodisia and Nikarion and Apollonia the Younger, my five children by Apollonia also known as Semmonthis [*sic*], with whom I live as my lawful wife; and they are to possess for their households the [above-mentioned] two female slaves and the cow in equal shares, according to the division I have made. Esthladas is to set aside in the open lot given him facing his door to the west a space of four square cubits for an oven. My other buildings and open lots, in Great Diospolis . . . , Esthladas is to have in half share, and Apollonia and her sisters in half share, and all my remaining assets—outstanding loans in kind and in money, and all furniture—in half shares. Esthladas and Apollonia (acting for herself and her sisters) are jointly to pay the expenses of building the dovecote on the planned site till they complete it. And for four years to my wife Apollonia also known as Semmonthis, if she lives blamelessly in the house, they are to give for the maintenance of herself and her two [next oldest] daughters each month 2½ artabs of wheat, ¹⁄₁₂ of castor beans, and 200 copper drachmas. And after the four years they are to give at their joint expense the same measures to the two younger daughters for eleven years. And they are to give to [Aphrodisia also known as] Takhratis for a dowry twelve copper talents from their joint funds. Semmonthis is to retain possession of whatever properties she clearly acquired for herself whilst married to Dryton, and any proceeding against her for those [is to be null and void].[14]

That last sentence reminds us of something we saw above, namely how successful Apollonia/Senmonthis was at putting her idle cash and stores of food to work earning high interest. Obviously that business activity 'on the side' had brought her some not insignificant sums of money, some of which she had invested in various properties.

Between the date of that will and the time when he died, some fifteen years later, Dryton too acquired some additional property. To cite the most obvious example, he speaks in his will only of his land in the Pathyrite nome, but at the time of his death he also owned land in the adjacent Peritheban nome. While much of his property was divided among all his children, the will, despite the clumsiness of its expression in places, leaves no doubt about the disposition of the vine land and its appurtenances: Dryton left all that part of his estate entirely to Esthladas. (The first-born customarily got a larger share.) But not long after Dryton's death his five daughters appear (in the document quoted in the next paragraph) as half-owners of the landed property too. It is not hard to reconstruct what must have happened. Feeling that his father's will was less than fair to his half-sisters, that collectively they ought to share equally with him in everything (except, obviously, the military equipment), Esthladas deeded them half-ownership of the land after he inherited it. Whether his stepmother had a hand in leading him to that decision we shall never know. In the light of what we do already know about her ability and resolve, it is hard to imagine her standing idly by while her daughters were short-changed. But her role, if any, in the outcome is less significant than the outcome itself. Whether Esthladas acted spontaneously or in response to gentle suasion or to hysterical tantrums, his generous action in sharing the landed property is still another sign of the affectionate relationship in which he and his half-sisters had grown up together. His generosity was all the more noticeable to his contemporaries, in whose eyes he, as the first-born and only son, would have been without fault in receiving and retaining a larger share than the other children. Dryton, in other words, in leaving a larger share to Esthladas, was conforming to accepted practice.

The sisters' half-ownership of the land is revealed in the following document, which dates from between 113 and 111 BC.

To Phomous, 'king's cousin', epistrategos and strategos of the The-baid, from Apollonia also known as Senmouthis and Aphrodisia also known as Takhratis, both daughters of Dryton, residents of Pathyris. There belongs to us and to our sisters—Aristo also known as Sen-monthis, Nikarion also known as Thermouthis, and Apollonia the Younger also known as Senpelaia—a half share of the domestic slaves and the lands of our late father in the Peritheban and Pathyrite nomes. Among the lands there are at Kochlax on the Arabian [i.e. east] bank [of the Nile] in the said Pathyrite nome a half share of 2½ arouras, more or less, of vine land, and to the east of that a vegetable garden, water wells, a farmstead, a wine press, a piece of dry land, another piece of non-revenue-yielding land, and all their appurten-ances. Our father acquired these during his lifetime and we [acquired them] after this death, but Aristōn son of Athenodotos, of Great Diospolis, forcefully occupied the aforementioned vine land and its appurtenances at a time when travel between the two banks [of the river] was interrupted, and he now lays claim illegally to the half share devolving to us and he has planted a part to vines, making light of us because we are women and, living as we do in another place, we are not able easily to give our attention to the property referred to. Therefore, fleeing to you for refuge, we ask, if you please, that you summon him and investigate, and, if it is as we state, that you compel him to vacate the half share of vine land described by us and the plantings in it and the adjoining places, and also to compensate us for the crops he removed therefrom; and that you, as one who hates wickedness, condemn him for the violence he has committed, so that we may [thus] obtain redress. Farewell.[15]

After this, the family of Dryton fades rapidly from our purview. A document of 103 BC refers to a loan made by Esthladas in 'Egyptian- and Greek-language contracts'. Clearly the family was still well-to-do, and its money-making proclivities persisted in the next generation. Dryton had been dead some ten years then, but the canny Apollonia/Senmonthis may well have been alive yet: in 103 BC she would have been in her late fifties or early sixties. Next in chronological sequence come two ostraca, written in Krokodilopolis on 14 and 30 May 100 BC. They record tax payments, each of 1,000 drachmas, made by four of Dryton's five daughters. We have here another indication of the family's continuing wealth. Even more remarkable, however, is the fact that while these tax receipts are written in Greek, the women are identified only by their Egyptian names, Senmouthis, Thermouthis, Senmonthis, and Senpelaia. Those, obviously, were the names by which they were generally known and addressed locally, the names which they and their neighbours used in an area where nearly all the population were of Egyptian descent. For Dryton's daughters the principal survival of the Hellenic culture of their father's origins was the requisite use of the Greek language in dealings with agencies of government; their Greek may have got rusty through little use, but the evidence is clear that they never lost it completely. Beyond that, they lived their daily lives in the manner of the Egyptians all about them. To all outward appearances they had been, as we say of immigrants today, 'assimilated'. There remained one very important distinction, however: they never lost the superior, non-Egyptian legal status that Dryton's and Apollonia's Greek ancestry bestowed upon them.[16]

7
Upward Mobility in the Civil Service: Menkhes, Village Clerk

Time: *c.*120–110 BC for Menkhēs; to 99 BC for his two successors in office.

Place: Kerkeosiris, a small village near the larger Tebtynis, in the south-west corner of the Arsinoite nome (Map 2).

Documents: Published in *The Tebtunis Papyri* volumes I and IV, the archive comprises one Demotic and something above 150 Greek documents, including some three dozen papyrus rolls preserved in whole or in good part. Some of the rolls exceed four metres in length; one of them (*P. Teb.* 61), now measuring 4.21 metres, is revealed by its contents to have been originally about one-third longer. Most of the long rolls contain official records such as tax lists, crop reports, or surveys of the village lands. The Demotic document, two Greek complaints of assault (*P. Teb.* 128 and 129), and some fragments of land surveys and tax lists remain unpublished.

The papyri are now in the library of the University of California at Berkeley. The circumstances of their discovery are sufficiently unusual to warrant repeating them here. In the winter of 1899–1900, with funds provided by a wealthy Californian woman, B. P. Grenfell and A. S. Hunt—then two young Oxford dons, who were presently to become two of the most illustrious names in papyrology—began excavating the site of ancient Tebtynis. When results in the town proper proved disappointing, they moved on to the necropolis. What happened then is best told in Grenfell's own words:

The [Arsinoite] was the nome of the crocodile-god Sobk, who under various forms and names was worshipped in every village that could boast a temple of its own. In the Ptolemaic period, even after the extensive land reclamations from Lake Moeris, crocodiles must have still frequented the district in great numbers, and a pond or small lake full of the sacred animals was no doubt a common feature of the local shrines. An interesting account of the sacred crocodiles of the great temple of Sobk at Crocodilopolis, the capital of the nome, is given by Strabo, who came [there] soon after the Roman conquest. . . .

The tombs of the large necropolis adjoining the town [Tebtynis] proved in many instances to contain only crocodiles, and on Jan. 16, 1900—a day which was otherwise memorable for producing twenty-three early Ptolemaic mummies with papyrus cartonnage—one of our workmen, disgusted at finding a row of crocodiles where he expected sarcophagi, broke one of them in pieces and disclosed the surprising fact that the creature was wrapped in sheets of papyrus. As may be imagined, after this we dug out all the crocodile-tombs in the cemetery; and in the next few weeks several thousands of these animals were unearthed, of which a small proportion (about 2 per cent) contained papyri. The pits were all quite shallow, rarely exceeding a metre in depth, and the crocodiles were sometimes buried singly, often in groups of five or ten or even more, and with their heads generally to the north . . . The ordinary system was to stuff the mummy with reeds and sticks, which were covered with layers of cloth. . . . When papyrus was used, sheets of this material were wrapped once or several times round the mummy inside the cloth, to which the outer layer was often glued; and a roll or two would frequently be inserted in the throat or other cavities . . .

The most remarkable characteristic of the Greek papyri from crocodile-mummies is their great size. For enfolding crocodiles three or four metres in length small documents were useless, though they were employed as padding, in which case they had often not been unrolled or were hastily crushed together. For the outer layers the papyri used consisted of large unfolded rolls. . . .[1]

As with the cartonnage that yielded the Diophanes archive (Chapter 4), many of the papyri used to wrap and stuff those sacred crocodiles proved upon decipherment to be discarded official documents, in this instance from the files of the village clerks of Kerkeosiris in the last two decades of the second century BC.

Family tree: See Fig. 3.

A glance at the family tree tells us that we are in the presence of another family like that of Dryton's later marriage (Chapter 6). All of its members had (in the case of ——ynchis, presumably had) two names, one Greek the other Egyptian, but generally they used and were addressed by only one (the

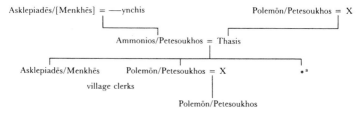

Fig. 3. Family tree of Menkhes

[a] The archive mentions three men, Ammonios, Herōdēs and Mousaios, any or all of whom may also have been sons of Ammonios/Petesoukhos and Thasis, that is brothers of the village clerks.

Egyptian most of the time), with both names being stated only in particular situations where formality required it. Furthermore, the Menkhes archive also brings us significant information about the legal status of such families. In one of the documents, a Greek translation (as it happens) of a Demotic contract that is not preserved, Menkhes and his father are styled 'Greeks born in this land', that is, they were natives of Egyptian stock who numbered among their male ancestors at least one who had emigrated to Ptolemaic Egypt from somewhere in the Greek world. Menkhes, and others like him, would thus be fully qualified by their background and upbringing to hold the office of village clerk, a post which required a knowledge of Greek, the language of government and most business activities, as well as of Egyptian, the language in which they would have to communicate with most of the local population.

We first encounter Menkhes in the year 119 BC, when he applied for reappointment to 'the office of komogrammateus [village clerk] previously held by me'. Nothing in the archive gives us any clue as to when Menkhes was born, but we may hazard the guess that at the time of his reappointment he was some thirty or more years old. The letter confirming his reappointment, written by the royal secretary of the nome to the regional officer who was Menkhes' immediate superior, is of more than passing interest:

Asklepiadēs to Marrēs, greeting. Menkhes has been designated by the finance minister for the village clerkship of Kerkeosiris, on condition that he work at his own expense ten arouras of the land reported as unproductive in the area of the village, at a rent of fifty artabs [of wheat] which, each year from the 52nd year on, he shall measure out to the Treasury in full or make up the deficiency from his own private means. Transmit to him this certificate of office, and see to it that the terms of his undertaking are fulfilled. Goodbye. Year 51, Mesore 3 [20 August 119 BC].[2]

This simple-sounding letter has ramifications far exceeding the mere reappointment of a village clerk. It also reveals, *inter alia*, one of the means employed by the royal administration for getting derelict and marginal lands back into cultivation. To understand those implications we must go back a quarter of a century.

Ptolemy VI, who died in 145 BC, left a son to succeed him. That son, ptolemy VII Eupatōr, never reigned. He was promptly assassinated and succeeded by his father's younger brother (p. 91), who now, as Ptolemy VIII, coolly assumed the surname of a second Euergetēs, 'benefactor' (but everyone called him Physkōn, 'pot-belly'). Thereafter, the intrigues by which Ptolemy VIII and Kleopatra II, his sister and first wife, sought to unseat each other erupted intermittently into armed conflicts (one of which, as we saw, called up Esthladas of Chapter 6 for active service). As Kleopatra had, generally speaking, the backing of the inhabitants of Alexandria and the Delta—Jews as well as Greeks—Ptolemy sought and obtained his chief support in the soldiery and native population of the up-country. At one point in the hostilities he exacted a brief vengeance in Alexandria by expelling the scholars of its famous Museum and organizing (at least this seems probable) the first recorded pogrom against the Jews of the city.

In the years just before 119 BC, the armed clashes between the two factions had reached a new peak of intensity, and the resulting conditions of insecurity had caused many farmers to flee for their safety, abandoning the land they were cultivating. In 118 BC the royal antagonists, both of them frustrated in their ambitions, agreed to a truce and attempted to restore calm by issuing a long series of decrees granting amnesty and various concessions. One of the latter was the following moratorium:

And they have decreed that cultivators of vine land or orchards in the interior, if they plant them between the 53rd and 57th years [118–113 BC] in the land which has become flooded or dry, shall be left untaxed for five years from the time of planting them, and from the sixth year for three years more they shall be required to pay less than the regular amount [of the tax], payment being made in the fourth year, but from the ninth year onward they shall all pay the same taxes as the other owners of productive land; and that cultivators in the territory of Alexandria shall be allowed an extra three years' grace.

Another of the decrees provides:

Neither strategoi nor [other] appointees to public office nor their subordinates nor any other person whatsoever shall fraudulently oust the cultivators from crown land that is in production, or reassign it to themselves to farm.[3]

In the area of Kerkeosiris these and other government stimuli to reclamation had only a modest degree of success. The extant papyri from Menkhes' office contain detailed records of plantings and yields on the crown lands for five of the harvests between 121 and 110 BC, and totals for five others. These reveal that the number of arouras sown and the rents derived therefrom by the Treasury declined from the year 121 TO 117 and then began to pick up, but only slightly. In 121 BC 1,308¾ arouras (including seventy-eight of reclaimed land) were sown, yielding a total rent, in all crops, of 5,274¹⁄₁₂ artabs. Those totals were never again attained during the dozen years of Menkhes' extant records. In the harvest of 117 BC those figures dropped to 1,139 arouras and 4,658¹⁄₁₂ artabs. Thereafter the totals, fluctuating slightly from year to year, climbed to around 1,200 arouras and 4,700 artabs. The best gain was achieved—where it was most desired—in the land sown to wheat: from a low of some 600 arouras (including forty-three reclaimed) yielding rents of some 2,600 artabs in 117, wheat production had by the year 110 risen to 702 arouras and 2,991¹⁄₁₆ artabs.

These figures reveal that not much more than a third of the available land was reclaimed during the years after the amnesties and concessions decreed in 118 BC. What is more, until 112 BC the loss from unproductive land at Kerkeosiris continued to exceed yields of the sown land. In 117 BC the land classified as unproductive amounted to 1,001⅛ arouras, which would have yielded 5,004¹¹⁄₁₂ artabs in rents. Four years later those losses in production had been reduced to 936½ arouras and 4,838¾ artabs. That year marked the first time that the rents actually collected from the crown lands of Kerkeosiris, a total of close to 4,700 artabs, exceeded the loss sustained from the lands still remaining out of production.

It is against the background provided by these data that the letter confirming Menkhes' reappointment conveys its full significance. The second of the royal decrees quoted above pointedly enjoined officials from using their positions of authority to snatch good lands from the peasants already cultivating them. The clear further implication of that decree, an implication which is confirmed in the authorization of Menkhes' reappointment, is that officials were encouraged, and in certain circumstances were actually required, to take on the responsibility for putting abandoned lands back into production. Moreover, the five artabs per aroura charged Menkhes was the highest rate of rental for crown lands, a rate normally collected on fields of prime quality. As we shall see presently, fields just being restored to cultivation after years of neglect were let to ordinary people, as an inducement, at a small fraction of the top rate, that is, one artab per aroura or even less. The premium rate charged Menkhes (and other officials like him) was no doubt a way of making him pay for an incumbency which, in addition to paying him a salary, could also be counted upon to engender lucrative perquisites. In the normal course of his duties, which included keeping the village's records and conducting its correspondence with officialdom, the village clerk was obviously in a singularly strategic position to render or deny many a favour to many a local inhabitant—by invoking or by obviating bureaucratic delay, to cite but one of many possibilities.

Menkhes, in turn, was similarly beholden to his superiors. Thus, in his bid for reappointment he offered to deliver not only the officially stipulated fifty artabs but also seven other quantities of varied produce totalling another fifty. Those 'voluntary' supplements sound for all the world like *douceurs* which Menkhes knew from experience would make the difference between the expedited approval and the possible rejection of his application.[4]

In the palmy days of the third century BC the Egyptian peasantry took up the proferred leases of crown lands on the whole willingly, at times even eagerly. The practice of assigning unworked crown land for compulsory cultivation was introduced in 164 BC, when the Ptolemaic regime faced the problem of how to restore production in the extensive areas that had been abandoned in the troubles and upheavals of the years immediately preceding. Once introduced, compulsory cultivation quickly became institutionalized, and by Menkhes' time, a half-century later, some of those compulsory leases had been made hereditary.[5]

For Menkhes, the obligation to cultivate those ten imposed arouras was no hardship. On the contrary, he appears to have conducted, while in office as village clerk, quite a successful agricultural business on the side. There is a record, for example, of a plot of 12¾ derelict arouras, ten of which were reclaimed by Menkhes in the year 113/2 BC after they had remained flooded for six or seven years. In the same year he took on twenty more waterlogged arouras, and ninety-three arouras of unproductive land. These last were the combined total of four plots held by four cleruchs, whose rent, by virtue of their privileged status, was set at a nominal one artab per aroura. Menkhes undertook to have the ninety-three arouras cultivated so as 'to produce the one-artab levy for the current year, or pay it out of my own pocket'. Since Menkhes, in order to hold his office, was prepared to pay five times that rate on other land registered as unproductive, it seems obvious that he looked forward to clearing a substantial profit on those ninety-three arouras. Then, too, there is a contract of the following year by which Menkhes leased from a cleruch ten arouras of land sown to grass, his intention apparently being to allow others, for a fee, to pasture their animals there. In yet another record we find Menkhes inscribed as the holder of two plots of land, presumably leased from the crown.[6]

It goes without saying that Menkhes did not cultivate all those fields—or, for that matter, any of them—by the sweat of his own brow. What is more, by virtue of his office, the repository of all the village records, he was in a better position than anyone else to know where to find the necessary manpower among the villagers (and no doubt to pressure them to work for him if they could not be persuaded by inducements). And there is every reason to suppose that a man who had held the office of village clerk for so many years as Menkhes had done, was canny enough to involve himself in such enterprises only when he saw the reasonable certainty of a tidy profit.

In 110 BC Menkhes was succeeded as village clerk by his brother Polemon. In the absence of evidence as to cause or motivation, the conventional supposition has been that the change occurred because Menkhes died or retired because of old age or infirmity. But as most and possibly all of the evidence just cited about his activities in agriculture dates from the last two years of his incumbency as village clerk, it becomes possible to entertain the suspicion that Menkhes arranged to transfer the office to his brother in order to free himself to concentrate on his profitable agricultural enterprise.

In the organizational scheme of the Ptolemaic government, the prime function of the village clerk was that of compiler and keeper of the basic records of the basis of the economy, agriculture. The records kept by Menkhes were of several types, relating to land, crops, population, rents, and taxes. His records were also multitudinous; scores have survived, comprising hundreds of columns of writing (the equivalent of our pages) on rolls and sheets of papyrus, and the survivors are but a fraction of the mountains of paper that must have crammed his office. Menkhes' records, as one recent writer put it, 'show in detail one aspect of the Ptolemaic administration with all its weaknesses and defects. The empirical nature of the system, the duplication of official responsibilities . . . and the supreme fiscal interest of the state all appear in clear relief'.[7] Let us now have a look at some of those records.

In the late summer and early autumn of each year, after the annual Nile flood had made it apparent which areas would be cultivable in the coming growing season, a land survey was carried out. The survey party consisted of a professional surveyor, the village clerk, and a number of other officials who acted as witnesses and certifiers. The resulting record was the village cadastre, on the basis of which the crops, rents, and

taxes were calculated. Following an age-old Egyptian custom
—one related, doubtless, to the direction of the flow of the
Nile—the cadastre recorded the results of the survey in a
south-to-north sequence. We also see from the Menkhes
papyri that the land survey gave rise to several types of
register. The briefest form merely listed, by localities, the
several plots of land identified by holder, category, and size.
The fullest form included, for each plot, the name of the
landholder, the rate of tax or rent, the measurements of the
four sides in *schoinia* and the resulting area in arouras, the crop
to be harvested therefrom, and the name of the cultivator.
Here is a brief extract from each of those two types:

Next on the south: beginning at the east, Petesoukhos son of Sarapiōn,
crown land 4½ [arouras]; next, to the west, an irrigation channel, ¼
[ar.] . . .
   Next on the west: beginning at the north, the 7-aroura *klēros* of
Komōn son of Pekhysis, [soldier] of Khomenis' unit, 6½ [ar.] . . .

Next on the west: beginning at the south, the 7-aroura *kleros* of
Kollouthes, [soldier] of Khomenis' unit,   6½ [ar.]
[plus] crown land   3¹/₃₂
                                       total   7¹⁵/₃₂
@ 4½ [art. per ar.]
                                    1³/₁₆
[measurements of the
   four sides, *schoinia*]   6²³/₃₂   6⁷/₃₂   = 8 [ar.]
                                    1⁵/₁₆
   excess ¹⁷/₃₂ [ar.]
   [crop] black cummin; cultivator, himself.[8]

We also learn from the last-quoted example how the area of
a quadrilateral was calculated in those days, at least for
government, if not scholarly, purposes. The averages of the
lengths of the opposite sides were simply multiplied, whether
or not the outline was rectangular. For a plot of land shaped
as in Fig. 4 the area was taken to be $(a + c)/2 \times (b + d)/2$. As
a result, the area thus calculated often exceeded the total
arrived at by actual measurement in the survey, as in the
example just quoted, where the calculation results in an
'excess' of just over half an aroura.
   Menkhes' work with the land survey was not finished when

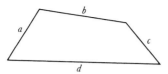

Fig. 4. Calculating the area of a quadrilateral

he had compiled those registers. He also had to prepare several types of supplementary lists. In one type he detailed, by categories, the names of the holders of temple and cleruchic lands and the number of arouras in each landholding. In another he compiled a similar list of the men cultivating crown land, showing how much land each held on lease individually or in partnership, the amount of the rent due, and the amount actually paid. In still another he recorded the quantities of crown land remaining unproductive, as in this extract:

Year 4 [113 BC], from Menkhes village clerk of Kerkeosiris. Report of unproductive land . . . reported to the finance minister after the sowing of year 4, and likewise that which can be brought under lease in year 5 at a nominal rent.
Turned unproductive in the years since year 40 [131 BC]: 340³⁄₁₆ [ar. formerly yielding rents of] 1,775⁵⁄₁₂ art.
Turned unproductive in the years through year 39: 596⁷⁄₁₆ [ditto] 3,063⁹⁄₁₆ art.
Total unproductive land: 936½ [ditto] 4,838¾ art. . . .
Less: unproductive land that can be brought under lease in year 5 at nominal rent for pasture and grass from the land turned unproductive since year 40, 30 ar. formerly yielding 141⁹⁄₁₆ art., to be let instead for five years @ ¼ [art./ar.], for five more years @ ½, and thereafter at 1.
Breakdown of those 30 ar.:
  watered by the flood in year 51 [120 BC],
    5¹¹⁄₁₆ [ar. yielding] 28¾ art.
  dry since year 40, 11¹⁄₁₆ [ditto] 45 [art.]
  unplanted and waste, 13¼ [ditto] 67⅚ art.,
  total, 30 ar. formerly yielding 141⁷⁄₁₂ art.[9]

After recording in such various forms the cadastral data derived from the land survey of each year, Menkhes kept track of the crops as the year progressed. Here again his records took several forms, varying from brief summaries to detailed itemizations. The following, for example, is an interim report which he prepared, probably for the royal secretary of the nome, on 9 November 114 BC, a time of the year when the Nile flood had mostly subsided and the sowing season had begun; the fact that this report is dated the 20th of the Egyptian month suggests that village clerks had to submit such statements every ten days, the 'week' into which those thirty-day months were sometimes divided.

Year 4, from Menkhes village clerk of Kerkeosiris. Report of irrigated and sown land as of Phaophi 20th.
In year 3 there had been planted 1,193¾ ar., yielding rents of 4,665⁵/₁₂ art. Of that there have been irrigated up to Phaophi 20th 1,122¼ ar. [yielding] 4,313⁵/₁₂ art. The balance, which the water still covers, is 71½ ar. [yielding] 351½ art.
Of the irrigated land there have been sown:

	[arouras]	[rent yield]
to lentils	9	44¼ art.
to chickling	35	167½ art.
to grass	60	60 art.

Balance on hand to be sown: 1,018¼ [ar. yielding] 4,042⅙ art.[10]

Apparently it was still too early in the agricultural year for planting the cereal crops, to which the bulk of the area would be given over. No doubt Menkhes continued to submit similarly detailed reports of plantings periodically—perhaps every ten days, as suggested above—until the sowing season was completed. Later in the year he would prepare a comparable series of reports detailing the rents actually collected (in contrast to those projected) from the several crops. Those reports fill the longest of the papyrus rolls found in the Tebtynis cemetery of the sacred crocodiles. They are much too long for any to be quoted here in full, as well as being (for us) monotonously repetitious. The following is one of Menkhes' briefer crop reports (ninety-eight lines of writing in five columns), drawn up after the earlier crops were in but giving only projections for wheat and barley, the harvesting of which was still in progress; in a subsequent report the figures for those cereal crops are different.

Year 53, from Menkhes village clerk of Kerkeosiris. Summary by crops of the said year. In year 52 there were sown, including pastures, 1,139¼ ar. of land, yielding rents of 4,642½ [art.], in the following anticipated breakdown: wheat 1,644⅔, barley equivalent to 2,877¼ in wheat, olyra equivalent to 91¾ in wheat, copper 39⁵⁄₁₂ [wheat equivalent], total expressed in wheat 4,642¹⁄₁₂ [art.]

For year 53 there have been sown:

to wheat, 576⅞ ar. yielding rents of 2,567⅓ art. [A breakdown follows showing the number of arouras of land in each of seven categories, in which the rents ranged from 2½ to 5 art./ar.]

to barley, 178⅜ ar. yielding rents of 787⅓ art. wheat equivalent, [then broken down into five categories with rents from 3 to 4¹¹⁄₁₂ art./ar.], total 1,312⅓ art. barley.

to lentils, 211 ar. yielding rents of 932⁵⁄₁₂ art. wheat equivalent, of which 151 ar. @ 4¹¹⁄₁₂ [art.] = 741¹¹⁄₁₂, 22 @ 4 = 88, 15 @ 3 = 45, 23 @ 2½ = 57½; less 432⁵⁄₁₂ art. included above under wheat land, balance of lentils = 500 art.

Total of above, expressed in wheat, 966¼ ar., 4,618⅔ art.

[There follows similar itemizations for greenstuffs—chickling, grass, cut hay, and standing hay.]

Total, including land sown to cereals, 1,122¼ ar., 4,658 art. [broken down as above, year 52].

This amount is collectable as follows: 3,331⅓ art. in wheat, 1,312⅓ in barley (equivalent to 787⅓ in wheat), 500 in lentils, and copper equivalent of 39⁵⁄₁₂ art. wheat; total expressed in wheat, 4,658¹⁄₁₂ art.

Also to be collected: rents on irrigated land left unsown through carelessness of the farmers listed below [five or more names], total 17 ar. . . . 83¾ art., wheat equivalent.

There is also the land sown in the area of the village after being reclaimed from unproductive under the supervision of Ptolemaios son of Philinos, 16½ ar. leased out without loan of seed to [three names] at a rent of 1 art. = 16½ art., divided thus: wheat 10, barley (to be paid in wheat) 2, fenugreek (to be paid in wheat) 4½.[11]

In separate reports Menkhes recorded rent yields according to categories of land or landholdings (temple land, cleruchic, crown, unproductive, reclaimed), and in some reports of that type the entries were further broken down to show the individual land parcels.

In short, Menkhes was responsible for keeping an eye on every stage of his village's agricultural progress and performance. In addition to compiling and submitting the many annual and seasonal reports sampled above, he had to act in particular situations as they arose. There is, for example, a document of 114/13 BC in which the village clerks are asked by a higher official to help choose men 'conspicuous for honesty and steadfastness' to be assigned the task of guarding the crops against loss to the Treasury. In another document of the same year Menkhes reports that the cultivators of crown land have gone on strike and taken asylum in a temple. The already mentioned amnesty decrees of 118 BC reconfirmed that right of asylum: 'And they have decreed that no one is to be taken out of the existing places of asylum on any pretext'.[12]

Although the agriculture of the village in all its ramifications occupied a large part of Menkhes' time, that was hardly the sole area of his responsibilities as village clerk. Let us now turn to look at some of his other concerns and activities.

Among the other duties that made the life of a village clerk a busy one there were the endless correspondence that his office entailed, and the frequent trips to be made on official business—locally for inspections of one kind or another, periodically (perhaps monthly) to the nome capital thirty kilometres away, and possibly even, on rare occasions, to Alexandria. His time and energies were claimed, too, by all sorts of contretemps which arose in the ordinary daily life of people living together in the same locality. In that connection there is a curious incident in which Menkhes was involved, an incident that cries out to be related here. Menkhes recounted the events in the following petition that he addressed to the reigning sovereigns (who happened to be travelling in the vicinity) in his own name and that of his brother Polemon.

On the 17th of Hathyr of the current 53rd year, when word reached us that Asklepiadēs, of the staff of Aminias, chief of the military police of the nome, was coming to the village, in accordance with custom we went to meet him, taking with us the headman of the village, some of the elders of the tenant farmers, Demetrios the chief constable and acting-chief of police of the village, and others. We greeted him, and he arrested us [Menkhes and Polemon] as well as Demetrios and one of the farmers, Marrēs son of Petōs, stating that there was entered against us as well as Marōn son of Diodoros, Petesoukhos son of ——, and Simōn son of ——, all of the said village, and also against Artemidoros, village clerk of Ibion-of-the-Twenty-Aroura-Holders, a complaint by Haryotēs son of Harsiēsis,

of Krokodilopolis, that when they were dining together at a tavern in the village they tried to make an end of him with poison. We were brought by Asklepiades before Aminias on the 19th of the said month, and the result of the inquiry (at which Ammenneus, the royal secretary [of the nome], was also present) was that we were forthwith released because of the other side's failure to appear. Wherefore, to forestall our ever again being harassed by the same charges being resurrected ... or being subjected to false charges and extortion for oversights in our reports relating to your interests, we have been driven to flee to you for refuge and we beg you, O gods most great and victorious, to allot to us too a portion of that succour which you vouchsafe to all, and, since we were declared innocent as a result of an official inquiry at which the royal secretary too was present, if it please you, to order that our petition be sent to Apollonios, 'king's cousin' and strategos, who pursuant to your wishes sees to it that no one can reinstitute proceedings from motives of calumny or extortion, and thus no one will be allowed hereafter to harass us over the same charges or annoy us on any pretext whatsoever, and thus Menkhes will be able to carry out the duties of his service to you without hindrance and we will have obtained succour from you for the rest of our lives. Farewell.
[From the royal secretariat] To Apollonios: If matters are as he asserts, see to it that they are not harrassed or annoyed.[13]

What are we to make of this commotion? Before attempting to answer that question let us note in passing that one of the accused, Simon, was the bearer of a Jewish name. From a contemporary papyrus we know that there was a synagogue at Krokodilopolis, the nome capital. That information came as no surprise: it had long been known that there were Jewish communities in the cities and major towns of Hellenistic Egypt. But the mention of Simon in the above-quoted document suggests that there were at least isolated Jewish families, if not whole communities, even in some of the smallest villages of the countryside. (Kerkeosiris has been estimated to have had a total population of some 1,500 souls in the years when Menkhes was its village clerk.)[14]

To return to the strange accusation of poisoning and the sudden collapse of the case, we should note, first of all, that in Ptolemaic Egypt such charges did not automatically lead to the imprisonment of the accused before trial. Another document in the Menkhes archive tells us, for example, of a villager of Kerkeosiris who, though 'accused of murder and other crimes', was allowed to live at home till notified to appear in court in the nome capital, and then he was given three days within which to comply with the summons.[15] In the case involving Menkhes there must have been a good deal more than meets the eye in the carefully worded petition that he submitted. The accused were arrested on the 17th and taken to the nome capital, where they were kept in gaol on the 18th, brought to trial on the 19th and released then and there when the accuser failed to appear in court. Had the accuser in the meantime recovered from his intestinal disturbance and decided that he had not, after all, been poisoned? In that case, why had he not withdrawn the complaint? Too disconcerted? Afraid of being 'shown up' in open court, perhaps even inviting punishment for filing a false charge? The doubts and unanswerable questions multiply so long as we assume that the original accusation was bona fide. It seems more likely, therefore, that we have before us a case of harassment from ulterior motives, with the village clerk as a particular target. Note, for example, Menkhes' references to extortion. Note, too, that after giving the list of persons arrested, Menkhes says that they, not including himself and his brother, were at the dinner where the poisoning allegedly took place. If that was the literal truth—and Menkhes would hardly weaken his case by misrepresenting a material fact that could easily be verified—then it does seem that the village clerk and his brother were included in the accusation with malice prepense. At all events, the whole episode is striking evidence of the fact that the post of village clerk was one in which the incumbent made enemies as well as friends.

This impression is confirmed by a report of another incident that occurred some four months later. A dozen individuals from various parts of the nome had been charged with corruption and peculation, and their respective village clerks had been instructed to prepare and submit inventories of the possessions of each of the accused. Although the papyrus is considerably mutilated, enough of the text is preserved to show us that Menkhes prepared his report with commendable thoroughness despite the obstacles which 'they' tried to place in his way.[16]

While the village clerk had no police powers (those were exercised by a local constabulary backed up by a military or quasi-military unit stationed somewhere in the area), it was to him that the villagers generally addressed their complaints 'for forwarding to the appropriate authorities'. The complaints and grievances found in the papyri of the Menkhes archive give us precious glimpses into the everyday life of an Egyptian village toward the end of the second century BC. Several examples will be quoted or summarized in the remaining pages of this chapter.

A petition of the year 113 BC speaks for itself. Another papyrus in the archive reveals that Apollodōros, the complainant, had had occasion to file a similar petition only a few months before; then as now, when compelled to buy products at artificially high monopolistic prices, many looked for ways to 'beat the system'. In the earlier instance, when Apollodoros went to investigate without a police escort, he was set upon by the suspect and thrown out of the house; seven days later, as he tells it,

when I met Sisoïs by the temple of Zeus here and wanted to have him arrested (as Ineilous, armed guard, and Trychambos [agent of the nome finance officer] were at hand), his brother Pausiris, a coolie, together with Bellēs, Demas, Marōn son of Takonnōs, and others whose names I do not know, hurled themselves upon us. Overpowering us, they rained repeated blows upon us with the cudgels they had, wounding my wife on the right hand and me similarly. The loss to my contract amounts to 10 copper talents . . .

Here, in full, is the later complaint, submitted a day or two after the events recounted:

From Apollodoros, concessionaire of the sale of oil and its tax collection in the village in year 4. My enterprise has been brought to naught by persons illegally bringing smuggled olive and castor oil into the village for black-market sale. On the 11th of Mecheir word was brought to me that a certain Thracian of [the village of] Kerkesēphis, whose name I do not know, had smuggled oil into the house where the shoemaker Petesoukhos lives and was selling it illegally to Thaēsis, who was staying in the same house, and to the gooseherd ——ios and his daughter, inhabitant of the said village. As you were away at the time, I immediately called the police chief and someone from the police guard to the aforementioned shoemaker's house.

There I found the Thracian inside, but the contraband had been hidden. We searched for it and found some . . . concealed by a hide and sheepskins belonging to the shoemaker. [Whilst we were thus occupied the Thracian] took to his heels, and the contraband oil [recovered by us amounted to only —— drachmas' worth], resulting in a net loss to me of 15 copper talents. I therefore submit this statement so that you may add your signature and forward it to the appropriate officials.

In what was then clearly the normal procedure, Menkhes kept the original submitted to him and dispatched to the royal secretary of the nome a verbatim copy prefaced by his own letter of transmittal.[17]

A dozen of the extant documents from Menkhes' office are complaints of breaking and entering, theft, or physical violence. One such complaint, that of Apollodoros, has been quoted in the preceding paragraph. Another, although addressed to the police chief, was found with Menkhes' papers; it relates to stolen documents, which the addressee was presumably asked to search for and recover (the papyrus is broken off at the bottom, so that the wording of the specific request is lost to us). The village clerk, as already mentioned, had no police authority, and his function with regard to such complaints, as in the example just quoted, was principally to forward a copy to the proper authorities. He was, however, as we saw earlier, authorized and often specifically instructed by higher authority to conduct investigations, and he could no doubt often be expected to settle local differences by himself, as the following instance suggests.

To Menkhes village clerk of Kerkeosiris, from Apollophanēs son of Dionysodōros, a crown-land farmer of the said village. On the 20th of Phaophi of year 5 Nikōn son of Amenneus, of the said village, released the water on his own land and flooded 2¼ ar. of the crown land for which I am responsible just as it was being ploughed. As a result my loss amounts to 20 art. wheat. I therefore submit [this complaint] to you, so that the accused may be summoned and compelled to reimburse me for the damage, and if he refuses [I request] you to send a copy of this complaint to the appropriate officials, so that I may have it recorded and the Treasury may suffer no loss. Farewell.[18]

As we have already seen in Chapters 1 and 4, the

coexistence in the same village of Egyptian peasants and Greek-descended cleruchs created a special area of tension that could turn ugly at slight provocation. Often, in fact, no provocation at all was needed, as the cleruchs, or at least some of them, regarded the peasants as fair game for victimization upon mere whim. There are five complaints addressed to Menkhes on the same day in 113 BC by five different Egyptian farmers against a rampaging cavalryman who, they protest, accompanied by other armed men broke down their front doors and ransacked their homes, carrying off what they pleased. Here is one of the five complaints.

To Menkhes village clerk of Kerkeosiris, from Harmiysis son of Sarapiōn, a crown-land farmer of the said village. On the 8th of Mesorē of year 4 my house was invaded by Pyrrhichos son of Dionysios, one of the cavalry colonists, and Herakleios son of Poseidippos, of the said village, together with very many others armed with swords. Forcing their way in they broke the lock of my mother's room and carried off the objects listed below, although I had done absolutely nothing to offend them. I therefore submit [this complaint] to you in order that you may add your signature regarding the details and forward a copy of the complaint to the authorities concerned, so that I may recover my property and they suffer the appropriate punishment. Farewell.

A woman's robe worth 1 talent 4,000 drachmas.
A woman's sleeved tunic worth 4,000 drachmas.
A jar containing 1,600 copper drachmas.[19]

Particularly poignant in the above is the remark 'although I had done absolutely nothing to offend him'; it evokes a picture of village life in which a cowed Egyptian community kept largely to itself, avoiding the Greeks, most especially the Greek soldiery, for fear of putting a foot wrong and thereby inviting wrath and ill treatment. Troubles of this sort within the village had their counterpart also in friction between villages. Especially frequent were disputes with people in an adjacent settlement named Berenikis Thesmophorou. They are repeatedly accused, in papers of the archive, of deliberately interfering with the irrigation works, to the detriment of farmers in Kerkeosiris. There is also the following complaint of cattle rustling; it dates from 110 BC, the year in which the village clerkship passed from Menkhes to his brother, to whom it is addressed (using, as with Menkhes, only his Egyptian name, even though it is written in Greek).

> To Petesoukhos village clerk of Kerkeosiris, from Hōros son of Konnōs, crown-land farmer of the said village. On the 20th of Thoth of year 8, as the forty sacred sheep belonging to the farmers of the said village and herded by me were grazing in the fields near Kerkeosiris, Petermouthis son of Kaoutis, a 20-aroura holder, and his brother Petesoukhos, a 7-aroura holder, and [three more names] together with others from Berenikis Thesmophorou set upon me like brigands and drove off a mixed herd of forty sheep, twelve of which were pregnant. I request that you forward a copy of this complaint to the authorities concerned in order that the culprits may be tracked down, the animals returned to me, and the assailants themselves suffer the appropriate punishment, and before all else that their landholdings be seized under lien to the Treasury. Farewell.[20]

Unlike Kleon of Chapter 2, whose surviving papers relate to his family and private life as well as to his activities in office, Menkhes is revealed to us almost exclusively in his official capacity. The family tree at the head of this chapter is traceable only because the ordinary form of nomenclature in use in the Greek-speaking world was to identify individuals by name and patronym, that is A son of B, with the sometimes added detail of A's mother's name or B's father's. Only Menkhes' brother and father appear in the archive as other than such names of reference, and the latter only once. As already mentioned, we can only guess at Menkhes' age during his years in office. We may suppose that he married and had children, since most men did; but his archive of official papers breathes not a word about any such dependants. He was a man of property and business acumen—that we have already seen. What, if anything, can we infer about his level of literacy and culture? A small amount of indirect evidence may enable us to answer that question, at least to a degree.

In 110 BC Menkhes was succeeded as village clerk by his brother Polemon/Petesoukhos, who held the office for three years and was in turn succeeded by a man whose name remains unknown to us. A study of the handwriting has led one scholar to suggest, quite recently, that Nos. 1 and 2 of *The Tebtunis Papyri*, extracts from anthologies of Greek verse on love and nature, were written by that anonymous village clerk. Being literary papyri, they are written in a book hand: the individual letters—uncials with a few cursive influences—are set down with grace and regularity by an obviously skilled penman to create a page of beauty and elegance.[21]

What, if anything, does that tell us about Menkhes? In later centuries, when Egypt was a province of the Roman Empire, the office of village clerk was transformed into an unsalaried compulsory public service, and we have evidence that men were sometimes assigned to that duty who could barely manage to sign their names; the real paper work, even for literate office-holders, was performed by clerks or professional scribes hired by the incumbents. The conditions that obtained under the Ptolemies were very different. The salary, status, and authority that went with the office of village clerk made it a sought-after post; Menkhes, as we saw at the beginning of this chapter, bid a substantial sum to have his appointment renewed. Under such conditions the government would not need to scrape the manpower barrel for less than fully qualified personnel. In all likelihood, therefore, some of the papers in the Menkhes archive were written by Menkhes himself, but no one has yet succeeded in singling out those papyri in the great mass of the archive.

Although the evidence just adduced is indirect and round-about, it contributes its mite to supporting the logical assumption that Menkhes and his compeers were literate individuals. Perhaps only a few could emulate the handsome writing of *P. Teb.* 1 and 2, but all could read and write. What is more, as scions of Graeco-Egyptian families of substance and standing, most of them, if not all, must have belonged to that small segment of the population that was literate in the languages of both cultures. Such a person was Menkhes, and such another was Dionysios, to whom we turn next.

8
Upward Mobility in the Military Services

1. Dionysios Son of Kephalas

Time: 117–103 BC (There is one document of 139, a petition submitted by Dionysios' father. Its preservation with his son's papers may be explained by the fact that the back of the papyrus was later used, presumably by Dionysios, for jotting down a list of objects.)

Place: Akōris—also called Tēnis (present-day Tehneh in Middle Egypt), and sometimes Krokodilopolis after the animal worshipped in the local cult—in the Mōchitēs toparchy of the Hermopolite nome. The name Tenis was the Greek spelling of the Egyptian word for the butte, or cliff, which overhangs the Nile at that point, a natural watchtower dominating both the river valley and the edge of the eastern desert. Throughout most of Egypt's history the successive rulers—Pharaohs, Ptolemies, Roman emperors—took advantage of the strategic site to make it one of their most heavily garrisoned fortresses.

Documents: Seven Demotic and thirty-three Greek papyri, plus a few small fragments, one of them Demotic, the rest Greek. Acquired almost intact by Théodore Reinach in the winter of 1901–2, the archive is preserved in Paris, in the papyrus collection of the Sorbonne. Two of the Greek papyri were incomplete when obtained by Reinach, and the missing pieces later turned up in the collection of the Hermitage in Leningrad. The entire archive has been republished in an exhaustive study by E. Boswinkel and P. W. Pestman, *Papyrologica Lugduno-Batavorum* XXII (Leiden, 1982; hereafter abbreviated *PLB*).

Family tree: See Fig. 5.

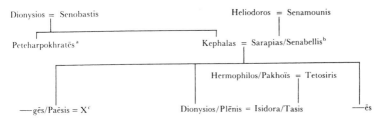

Fig. 5. Family tree of Dionysios son of Kephalas

^a Tothoēs and Petenouphis, who appear in the archive without further identification, may also have been sons of Dionysios and Senobastis.

^b Prior to 109 BC her Greek name is given as Demetria; nothing enlightens us as to the reason for the change of name. Her Egyptian name is also written Senabellous and Senabollous.

^c Sotionkhis who appears in the archive may have been Paesis' wife: see note 5, and the document cited there.

When we first encounter Dionysios, in 116 BC, he is some eighteen or twenty years old. By then he may already have been married; he certainly was a married man eight years later, when his wife first appears in the documents. Presumably they had some children, but, as will appear, the nature of the archive is such that there is no occasion for any to be mentioned.

Dionysios belonged to a family like those of Chapters 6 and 7, families with both Greek and Egyptian antecedents, as reflected in the dual names of the family members. The families of Dionysios and Drytōn were also alike in that some or all of their men, generation after generation, were professional soldiers. Unlike the cleruchs, who received allotments of land and lodgings for themselves and their families, these soldiers served in garrison units in exchange for pay and other emoluments. The soldier's life gave them status, leisure, and financial resources with which to acquire local properties and engage in other business dealings. They carried on these activities either themselves or through other family members, as we saw in the case of Drytōn and shall see again, in this chapter, in the case of Dionysios. In military— and consequently social—status, however, Dionysios' family was lower than that of Drytōn and his son Esthladas, who, it will be recalled, served in the cavalry, a corps from which natives of Egyptian or mixed ancestry were generally excluded. Dionysios and his father before him served in the infantry; his brother Paēsis, however, did manage to obtain promotion into the cavalry, evidence of one longstanding barrier beginning to give way.

In the last decades of the second century BC, Dryton's family, as we saw, was becoming increasingly assimilated into the Egyptian community within which it lived. In Dionysios' family the Egyptian element had been dominant since much earlier, perhaps as early as the beginning of the century. Still, they did not give up their Greek names or their ability to use the Greek language: they cherished those signs of their privileged status. Nevertheless, they were deeply immersed in the Egyptian cultural milieu: Dionysios, for example, even held a priestly office in the cult of the local ibis-god. The members of this family naturally used their Greek names in military, official, and most business affairs—contexts in which the language of the ruling power was either customary or required. But at home, and doubtless also in their intimate social relations, they called one another by their Egyptian names and spoke in the native tongue. On occasion they would even use Demotic when drawing up contracts with individuals bearing Greek names and patronyms, such as cavalrymen of the local garrison. But the criteria which determined that Demotic rather than Greek would be used in such circumstances remain a mystery to us.

Dionysios' upbringing was evidently bilingual. Several of the documents in the archive show how well he could write Greek, his handwriting as neat and skilled as that of any professional scribe. And he was also competent in the Egyptian language and its Demotic script, a scribal skill which he must have acquired either at home or in the Egyptian temple in which he served. It was an 'underclass' skill that few who prided themselves on their Greek descent would stoop to acquiring, the more so as it required assiduous application and led to no great career opportunities.

As sons of an army man, Dionysios and his brother Paesis enjoyed a right to follow in the same career as their father, and in due course we find them serving together under the same command. Apparently, however, the Akoris garrison was kept at full strength in those days after the recent internal troubles (Chapter 7), so that candidates such as Dionysios had to wait for an opening to develop before they could be admitted to the ranks. Until his enrolment Dionysios, and every other young man similarly situated, was officially styled, in Demotic at least, 'son of a mercenary soldier'. A document of 109 BC reveals that Paesis, the older brother, was then already in the army; how much earlier he was admitted we cannot tell. In the army Paesis' ethnic designation was that of Libyan, but his brother, we are surprised to find, is called Greek in a Demotic document and Macedonian in a Greek document. Even if the last two were merely loose variants of the same ethnic—which is far from certain—only one, if any, of the three can truly point to the part of the world whence one of their male ancestors migrated to Egypt. The other ethnic or ethnics must have been assigned upon enrolment in the military unit (p. 31). Unfortunately, we have no clue, either in this archive or elsewhere, as to what determined such assignments.

What did Dionysios do in his adult years before he was enrolled in his military unit? A minor priestly office which he held claimed a certain amount of his time and provided him with some income. But most of his time and effort was concentrated upon the land and its produce, and his involvement in agricultural and related enterprises did not end with his entrance into the armed forces. He appears to have acquired possession of some parcels of land as investments, and he took others on lease from the temple and the crown. Beyond a mention that two of the temple fields added up to eighteen arouras, nothing, however, helps us to judge the scale of his land operations.

When he took crown lands on lease, Dionysios *ipso facto* became a 'crown farmer', a term which generally conjures up the image of an Egyptian peasant struggling to eke out a bare subsistence. But it is obvious from the documents of the archive that Dionysios was no humble peasant. Like many another soldier or cleruch who obtained an income from the land, and like Menkhēs of Chapter 7, Dionysios left the back-breaking labour in the fields to others. Although he remained the owner or the lessee-of-record, his actual role was one of minimal physical exertion, mainly managerial. For the most part he had merely to contract with farmers to till his fields, keep an eye on their doings, and collect his rent at harvest time. Dionysios, like Menkhes, seems to have prospered in that role. In addition, Dionysios appears to have conducted an active business in agricultural loans, as the following evidence suggests.

The Dionysios archive includes petitions, leases, sales, receipts, and accounts, but two-thirds of all the documents concern the loans taken at frequent intervals, year after year, by Dionysios acting either alone or jointly with his mother and/or his wife. All the loans involve quantities of grain, ranging from 15 to 250 artabs. In all but three instances the loan was made in grain and was repayable in kind; in the three exceptions the loan was made in money, to be repaid in grain. Four of the loan contracts claim special mention here. On 9 January 105 BC Dionysios signed a loan for twenty-four artabs; the next day, together with his wife and mother, he acknowledged a debt of like amount to the same lender. The coincidences make it hard to think of these as two discrete loans. Yet, if they represent a single loan for which the two women became co-signers, why was the contract of the 9th not torn up, or at least invalidated by reference? Even more curious is the pair of loans taken on 16 December 108 BC. In one, a Greek contract, Dionysios acknowledged a debt of fifty artabs. According to the other, written in Demotic, his wife and mother on the same day borrowed the same amount from the same lender. Do the two contracts represent a total borrowing of 100 artabs, or only of fifty? Presumably the former, but a shadow of uncertainty remains. And why was one of the contracts drawn up in Demotic? It is not that the two women could handle only the Egyptian language, for they appear in several of the Greek contracts. Again the documents themselves do not provide an answer to the question, but the solution may lie in a legal technicality which we know about from another, contemporary source. In Chapter 4 we saw repeated references to 'the appropriate tribunal'. Ptolemaic Egypt had separate courts and judges for the application of Greek and native law, and the venue in any given case was

determined by a principle enunciated in one of the long series
of royal decrees of 118 BC (p. 107):

> They have likewise decreed with regard to lawsuits in which Egyptians
> and Greeks are opposed, that is suits brought by Greeks against
> Egyptians or by Egyptians against Greeks . . . that Egyptians who
> have entered into contracts with Greeks in the Greek language shall
> sue and be sued before the *chrēmatistai* [Greek circuit-judges], but
> those who, even though enjoying Greek status, have entered into
> contracts written in the Egyptian language [Demotic] shall be sued
> before the *laokritai* ['people's judges'] in accordance with the law of
> the land.

The texts of the two contracts, Greek and Demotic, will be
found at the end of this section on Dionysios.[1]

In all, the archive contains some two dozen loans spread
over a dozen years, and it is surely not unlikely that there were
quite a few other such contracts which have not survived.
Devoid of circumstantial detail, this bald recital of numbers
could suggest that Dionysios was indeed a hard-pressed
farmer saddled with debt upon debt as he struggled to make
ends meet. But a closer examination of details reveals that the
amounts of these loans exceeded, many times over, what
Dionysios would have required for feeding even a numerous
family in addition to sowing a sizeable landholding. Supposing
his family to have come to five or six souls, his requirement for
feeding them, figured not at a basic but at a lavish rate of
consumption, would not have exceeded 100 artabs a year. He
received, as it happens, that very amount in the annual rent
from the eighteen arouras which he had on lease from the
temple and subleased out to those who did the actual
cultivation. For sowing his fields he needed but one artab per
aroura. Yet his annual borrowing, to judge from the years best
attested, added up to debts of 300 artabs and more.

It is instructive, too, to consider the status of the creditors
from whom Dionysios borrowed. Two of them have, like
Dionysios himself, Greek and Egyptian names, and all the rest
have only Greek names and patronyms. With the possible
(but unlikely) exception of three whose occupation is un-
identifiable, they were all military men or cleruchs of the
vicinity. That fact helps us to fill out the picture of Dionysios'

business in loans. Clearly, his creditors were well-to-do men who acquired surpluses of grain from their farm operations and were happy to lend, from those otherwise idle surpluses, amounts of grain which would be repaid in kind at the next harvest increased by half, the standard rate of interest on loans in kind. From their repeated loans to Dionysios two inferences seem justified: that Dionysios, belonging to their own military milieu, was someone they considered reliable; and that they were therefore more than ready to do business with him on a steady basis, as it saved them the trouble and worry of having to look further for other borrowers, and possibly having to deal with strangers, an unknown element of risk.

The image of Dionysios that now emerges is hardly that of a hard-pressed peasant, piling loan upon loan in a frantic effort to keep his head above water, but rather that of a man who was making a very good thing out of an agriculture-related enterprise in which his hands were never dirtied by contact with the soil. The fields he owned or leased were farmed by others; and the likeliest explanation of his loan activities is that he kept borrowing other people's grain and cash as a means of turning a profit, which he could do by making loans at exorbitant interest rates to really needy peasants, and by selling grain on the open market to take advantage of seasonal fluctuations in the price. These impressions of Dionysios as a shrewd manipulator are further strengthened when we observe how regularly he managed, without suffering the stipulated penalty, to delay the repayment of his own borrowings by anything from one to five months. Here is a particularly instructive case in point.[2]

To Asklepiadēs, 'king's cousin' and strategos, from Dionysios son of Kephalas, one of the crown tenants of the village of Tēnis also known as Akōris of the Mōchitēs [toparchy]. For reasons which will appear in [this account of] the affair, my mother Senabollous and I executed through the registry in favour of Admētos also known as Khesthōtēs, of the same village, a contract of loan for 150 artabs of wheat in year 9 [109/8 BC]. Not only that, but in good faith I drew up in his favour a deed of mortgage on vacant lots that I own. The accused, once in possession of the contracts, carried out none of the terms agreed to between him and me, and as a result I suffered no small damage because of him. And even now he adopts an unjust stance and, observing that I am occupied with the sowing of the land I farm, he keeps annoying me and doesn't let me attend to my farming, in violation of the frequent royal edicts regarding us crown tenants. Therefore, as the land is in danger of going unattended and I am unable under present circumstances to take him to court over the contracts, I am forced to flee to you for refuge. I beg you, if you see fit, first and foremost to send an order to the police chief of Akoris not to allow the accused to interfere with me or my mother, and to give me guarantees [to that effect] in writing, until I am finished with the sowing and can settle accounts with him on all matters. If that is done, nothing of utility to the king will be lost, and I will have been protected. Farewell.

[From the strategos to the police chief] To Bias: If he is a crown tenant, see to it that he is left undisturbed until he has finished his planting. Year 10 Thoth 24 [12 October 108 BC].

Eighteen days later, with the sowing in full swing, Dionysios wrote again on the same matter, this time to the royal secretaries of the nome, citing the above and asking for their protection against being turned over to the officers who took charge of defaulting debtors. One of the royal ordinances proclaiming such protection for crown tenants is, as it happens, preserved among the decrees of 118 BC. It reads: 'And they have decreed that the [officers in charge] shall not on any pretext seize crown tenants or government employees[?] or others exempted by previous decrees from being hauled into court, but execution of debts in their cases shall be made upon their other property not protected by this decree'.[3]

Petitions like the one just quoted are, by their very nature, usually couched in pitiful language. In this instance, by charging his creditor with repeated (but unspecified) improprieties, Dionysios throws a smoke-screen around the fact that it is now October and he has not yet repaid a loan which was due in June/July. Now, as October was in the heart of the sowing season, he manages to defer payment still further by taking advantage of the royal injunction protecting crown tenants against distraction, by legal process or otherwise, from their prime function of planting their (that is, the king's) fields. There is no escaping the conclusion that Dionysios was a master of sharp practice, who knew where the loopholes were and how to profit from them. Another document in the archive reveals that he did not pay off Admetos until 19 December, and that he did so not out of his own pocket but by borrowing the requisite quantity of grain from someone else.

There is yet another good example in the archive of how quick Dionysios was to take advantage of every available subterfuge. His earliest recorded loan was taken some time in regnal year 54 [117/6 BC], and in the normal course of events, repayment would have been due at the harvest of that year, that is in June/July of 116. Before then, however, the lender disappeared without a trace. Just when his grass widow began to demand repayment of the loan we do not know, but since it could not be established that the lender was or was not dead, and since the wife apparently was unable to produce a copy of the loan document, obtaining indefinite postponements was mere child's play for our cunning Dionysios. At all events, it was not until September/October of 111 BC, sixty-three months after the due date, that Dionysios finally consented to repay the loan to the woman in exchange for her receipt, including the iron-clad formulary guarantee that

neither [the lender] himself nor anyone in his behalf shall proceed against Dionysios for the said loan (written in two copies) or any part thereof on any pretext whatsoever. If anyone does so proceed, not only is the suit to be ineffectual for [the lender] and for anyone claiming in his behalf, but also, for having brought the claim he is to pay to Dionysios a fine of five copper talents and costs, and this instrument is to remain nonetheless valid everywhere it is produced.[4]

The comfortable existence of Dionysios' family is glimpsed in the following complaint filed by his brother Paesis. We may wonder, in passing, why it turned up amongst Dionysios' papers. The answer may be that as Paesis was already in military service he left this copy with his younger brother, who, still a civilian, could more easily pursue the matter with the appropriate civil authorities.

To Nikanor and the other constables of [the village of] Kirka, from Paesis (also known as ——ges) son of Kephalas, inhabitant of Akoris, Libyan, one of the cavalrymen of Demetrios' troop. On the night leading to the 14th of Hathyr of year 9, certain parties broke like robbers into the abode belonging to me near the said village, stripped the clothes off the people living there, and went off with the

farm implements and the rest of what was there, a detailed list of which is given below. Now, as I suspect that the attack was the work of Kōnnōs, who comes from the Kynopolite nome but is now living in the village of Aithōn, and of others whose names I do not know, I submit this complaint to you so that the guilty may be searched out and sent off to the strategos, and thus the missing objects will be restored to me and the guilty will suffer the consequences. When that is done I will . . . Farewell. Year 9 Hathyr 16 [3 December 109 BC].
Itemized list:
[property] of Sotionkhis: a tunic, a cloak and a sack
Plēnis, my brother: a tunic, 1 plough, 1 yoke
Paptytis: a tunic and a sack
and guests: cloaks.[5]

The easy, not to say affluent, circumstances of Dionysios and his family are reflected in several other documents in the archive. In one contract, written in Demotic, Dionysios rents a team of female oxen and their young for the ultimate purpose of helping to bring in the harvest, which is still a half-year into the future. In return for the use of the animals he agrees to feed them for the duration of the contract (beginning at once), and to pay ten artabs of wheat at harvest time. That amount of wheat was a person's basic food requirement for a whole year. In two more of the Demotic contracts, one dated just before the other just after he entered the military service, Dionysios buys two cows, and again his disbursements were not insubstantial. Here, for example, is the second of those contracts; the figure in the penalty clause implies a purchase price (which is not stated—a practice rooted, no doubt, in the age-old Egyptian barter economy) of some 10,000 copper drachmas, a sum which would at that time have bought up to fifteen artabs of wheat.

Year 12 which has been equated with year 9, second month of the inundation season, under the monarchs Kleopatra, the goddess benefactress, and Ptolemy her son, who is called Alexandros, the god who loves his mother, and under the [eponymous] priest in Alexandria.
    Declared by the police chief of . . . , Psenamounis son of Abykis, his mother being Thermouthas, to the Greek Dionysios son of Kephalas, one of the soldiers [serving under the command] of Demetrios:
    'You have satisfied my heart with the money for the black cow,

which is sturdy on her feet, branded on the neck, able to lie down and get up, and is unhurt by any fall. I have given her to you for money and she belongs to you from today for all future time. . . . As for anyone who comes against you for her, I will take steps so that he goes away from you; otherwise I will give you 750 [deben] of silver—half is 375, which, again, makes [the total] 750—[paid] in copper . . . as a money penalty, in the month involved, perforce and without delay, beside the fact that I will still act so that you are left alone with regard to [the cow]. I will not be able to say, "This is not at all the cow which is described above, which I gave you for money." You are the one who has the right over me with regard to her, for it is indeed she, and I will act so that she remains free for you against [all claims], in keeping with what is written here above.'
Written by Pebes[?] son of Phibis . . . scribe of legal documents of the sacred[?] books of Thot, thrice great, master of Hermopolis, the great god.
[In Greek] Year 12 which is also year 9 Phaophi 15 [2 November 106 BC], at Ammonopolis. [Recorded] by Hermias.[6]

Because they are so uniformly concerned with business matters, the papyri of the Dionysios archive leave us uninformed in several areas where information would be very welcome. They tell us, for instance, next to nothing about the people in Dionysios' family. Of most of those whom we encounter we obtain their names and little else. His older brother, as we have already seen, entered the army first, got into the cavalry, and owned a house which was robbed. So much for him. Dionysios' mother and wife were co-signers of some of the loans which he took. So much for them. The rest is silence. Children and slaves, if any, never appear.

So, too, with Dionysios' priesthood: a mere mention and nothing more. The archive's lack of information on this subject is especially frustrating, because details of his priestly rank, role, and responsibilities would be uniquely enlightening on this Egyptian element in the life of a military family living approximately midway between Alexandria and Egypt's southern frontier at the end of the second century BC; a family, like so many others, whose service in the Ptolemaic armed forces presumably began with the immigration of a Greek or Macedonian ancestor some time in the third century BC.

The Greeks never developed a priestly class in their Aegean homeland. In the cities of classical Greece 'priestly office

[was] open to every man,' as the orator Isokrates explained to the king of Cyprus. In Egypt, in contrast, a clergy is in evidence from earliest historical times, called into being, no doubt, by the need for an organized worship of the Pharaoh, a god-king. The clergy, their temples endowed with treasure, rich ornament, and landed estates, became—especially in major centres such as Thebes and Memphis, with their vast complexes of impressive structures—great powers in their own right. As such, and as servants of a transcendent god from whom the Pharaoh's own powers derived, the priesthoods in the course of Egypt's millennial history were ever ready to challenge and supersede the royal power whenever it showed signs of decline. The priesthoods' latent hostility to the king not only continued under the Ptolemies but was exacerbated by the fact that the rulers were now foreigners. We know of ten revolts which occurred during the years of Ptolemaic rule. One of them was essentially the result of dynastic intrigue at the royal court, and was more or less confined to Alexandria. One or two others were basically of similar origin. The rest, sparked by economic grievance or governmental crisis, were native revolts against the royal power, with priests prominent in their leadership.

Thus, profoundly rooted in the native tradition of the country and alien to that of the Greeks, the professional priesthoods of the Egyptian gods remained all through the centuries of Ptolemaic rule the one element of society least infiltrated by Hellenic influence or personnel (see Chapter 5). Of all the priests and priestesses of Egyptian cults recorded in extant documents—the documents themselves written or inscribed preponderantly in the Egyptian language—only a very few have Greek names, and in many, if not all, instances, those men and women may also have had Egyptian names which happen not to appear in the sources. As a counterpart to that situation, there was a total exclusion of Egyptians from the Greek cult-offices, as we shall see in detail in a moment. Of the priestly office held by Dionysios we learn from the archive no more than this: in two of the Demotic papyri Dionysios is called by his Egyptian name, Plēnis, and by a name or epithet derived from the ibis-god he served, but his connection with the cult is not further described or detailed. A host of questions comes to mind. When did Dionysios enter the priestly office? How did he obtain it—through inheritance, intermarriage, purchase, or other means? What were the qualifications for the office, and what were its emoluments? All these and other questions remain hanging without answers, because the surviving papyri happen to relate mainly to the commercial side of Dionysios' life and reveal, incidentally, the merest scraps of its social side.

Dominated by monarchies in lieu of the city-states of classical times, the Hellenistic world did introduce one major change into the religious practices of the Greeks. When the Hellenistic rulers, following the lead of Alexander the Great, adopted the trappings of divinized monarchy, there quickly arose, as there had in the earlier Oriental monarchies, a need for a priesthood to serve the royal cult. In keeping with Greek tradition, however, there was never any thought of making this Hellenistic priesthood into a lifetime career, or its holders into a permanent, hereditary caste. These priests and priestesses were appointed by the ruler and held office at his or her pleasure; the office was honorific and political first, religious second. In Athens, the leading civil official was called the 'eponymous' archon, because the calendar year in which he served was designated by his name. In Ptolemaic Egypt, as we have already seen in numerous examples, years were designated essentially by their progression in a ruler's reign, year 1, 2, 3, etc. But in some documents of Ptolemaic date the year was further identified by adding the names of the eponymous priests and priestesses currently serving the cults of the several kings and queens of the dynasty, beginning with Alexander the Great. In addition to providing us with valuable chronological data, the eponymous dating affords another striking illustration of the discrete coexistence of the two cultures and their resistance to interpenetration. We noted above that with few, if any, exceptions, the priesthoods of the Egyptian gods were filled only by Egyptians. Similarly on the Greek side, extant records enable us to identify some 350 eponymous priests of the royal cults between 290 and 83 BC, and not a single one of them bears an Egyptian name. (To be sure, a few instances from the later years of Ptolemaic rule give rise to the suspicion—but in the present state of the evidence it can be no more than that—that the name was a Greek translation of an Egyptian name borne by a Hellenizing native.)

By Dionysios' time the eponymous formula had, through its recitation of so many separate rulers and gods, become so unwieldly that it had become a common practice to continue listing the cults but to omit the names of the individual priests and priestesses. These office-holders were thus eliminated as elements of the date, whilst the formula still celebrated the ruler-gods of the royal cults. Two contracts, one Greek, the other Demotic, recording a loan or loans taken on the same day by Dionysios and his mother and wife, illustrate this 'streamlined' listing of the cults while providing us with a fitting close to the story of Dionysios. To quote them in full will also serve to show the contrast between the Greek and the Egyptian way of recording the same or similar transactions. In the Greek, which is given first, the text runs to forty-one lines of writing, of which the first fifteen are taken up by the elaborate opening formula in its 'streamlined' style. In the Demotic, twenty-one lines in length, the formula occupies the first six lines. The date of both documents corresponds to 16 December 108 BC.

[Greek]

When Kleopatra and Ptolemy, gods *philomētores sōtēres*, were reigning, year 10, when the incumbent in Alexandria was priest of Alexander [the Great], of the gods *sōtēres*, the gods *adelphoi*, the gods *euergetai*, the gods *philopatores*, the gods *epiphaneis*, the god *eupatōr*, the god *philomētōr*, the god *neos philopatōr*, the god *euergetēs*, the gods *philomētores sōtēres*,[7] when also in function were the sacred priest of Isis great mother of gods, the wreath-bearer of Queen Kleopatra goddess *philomētōr sōteira dikaiosynē nikēphoros*, the prize-bearer of Berenikē *euergetis*, the torch-bearer of Queen Kleopatra goddess *philomētōr sōteira dikaiosynē nikēphoros*, the basket-carrier of Arsinoē *philadelphos*, the priestess of Queen Kleopatra goddess *philomētōr sōteira dikaiosynē nikēphoros*, the priestess of Arsinoē *philopatōr*, the incumbent priests and priestesses in Alexandria, month of Audnaios twenty-ninth Hathyr twenty-ninth, at Krokodilopolis also called Akoris, in the Mochites toparchy, Hermopolite nome.

Dionysios son of Asklepiadēs, Persian [by descendance], one of the cavalry colonists [under the command] of Apollophanēs and Apollonios, has loaned to Dionysios son of Kephalas . . . thirty-three and a third artabs of wheat, solidly packed, which [the borrower] has received from his store at home, at interest of one-half, viz. sixteen and two-thirds artabs. The borrower will repay the wheat and the interest, fifty artabs in all, to Dionysios or his representatives in the month of Lōios, which is Payni, of the current tenth year, in wheat [that is] new, clean and unadulterated, using a measure conforming to the [standard] bronze one and an honest strickle, delivered at the river-port for Akōris at his own expense, without litigation, judgement or trickery of any kind. If he does not repay as written, he is to forfeit as the price of each artab three thousand copper drachmas, not a whit less,[8] and Dionysios [the lender] and his representatives are to have the right of execution upon the borrower himself and upon all his possessions for the wheat and for everything in this contract, exactly as would result from a lawsuit. This contract is valid everywhere it is produced. Witnesses: [six are listed, all with Greek names and patronyms]. Contract in custody of [the lender].

[2nd hand] I, Dionysios son of Kephalas . . . have the fifty artabs as aforesaid, and I have given the original [of the contract] to Dionysios.

[3rd hand] I, Dionysios, have the original.

[4th hand] Year 10 Hathyr 29 in the village of Tēnis also called Akōris of the Mōchitēs. Registered by Ptolemaios.

[Demotic]

Year 10 third month of the inundation season, day 29, under the monarchs Kleopatra and Ptolemy, the gods who love their mother and save, and under the priest of Alexander, of the gods who save, of the gods brother and sister, of the gods benefactors, of the gods who love their father, of the gods manifest, of the god who ennobles his father,[9] of the god who loves his mother, of the god who loves his father, of the god benefactor, and of the gods who love their mother and save, and under the [other] priests in Alexandria.

Declared by the woman Senabollous daughter of Herieus, her mother being Senamounis, and the woman Tasis daughter of Pakhoïs, her mother being Tetosiris, two women speaking with one voice, to the cavalryman of the squadron of Apollophanēs, Dionysios son of Asklepiadēs:

'To you belong 50 artabs of wheat—[half is] 25, which, again, makes [the total] 50—[which are] with us as a debt of a capital [loaned] at interest. We will give it to you [at harvest time] in year 10 second month of the summer season, last day, [measured] by the bronze measure, in wheat [that is] choice, good, cleansed and without foreign element, and delivered at the wharf at Tēnis free of transport charges or any claim in the world. As for anything of this that we shall not have given you in year 10, second month of the summer season, in conformity with what is written above, we will give it to you each time as 150 deben of silver—[half is] 75 silver, which, again, makes [the total] 150 silver— paid in copper . . . per artab of wheat in the following month, perforce and without delay. Everything that belongs to us and that we shall acquire constitutes the guarantee of [your] right, in keeping with what is written. You will be able to compel whichever one of us you wish to behave toward you in conformity with every word which is here above. We will not be able to say, "We have [already] given you the wheat which is here above, we have filled [our] obligation to you in keeping with the document which is here above," so long as the document which is here above is in your hands.'

Written by Pekysis son of Harphaphaïs, who writes in the name of the priests of [the god] Thot.

[In Greek] Year 10 Hathyr 29 in Tenis of the Mochites. Registered by Ptolemaios.[10]

2.   Peteharsemtheus son of Panebkhounis

Time: 145–88 BC, embracing five generations of the family.

Place: Pathyris and Krokodilopolis, in Upper Egypt (Map 3).

Documents: The archive consists of papyri and ostraca, nineteen of them Demotic, fifty-one Greek, and two bilingual. Acquired on the antiquities market, the papyri and ostraca are scattered among collections in Berlin, Cairo, Fribourg, Heidelberg, Leipzig, London, Oxford, Strasbourg, and Uppsala. In type and contents they constitute the most varied of the archives studied in this book.

Family tree: See Fig. 6.

This family tree, embracing five generations, contains only Egyptian names. Some of the men in this family had careers in the armed forces. Hōros in the third generation of the table and Panebkhounis in the fourth were professional soldiers, and that Horos, we learn, served in the same unit as Dryton of Chapter 6. In one of the documents of the archive, Totoēs, the elder brother of that Horos, is styled 'a foreigner born in Egypt', and in the fifth generation Pelaias, who married a daughter of Panebkhounis, is described as 'a Greek born in

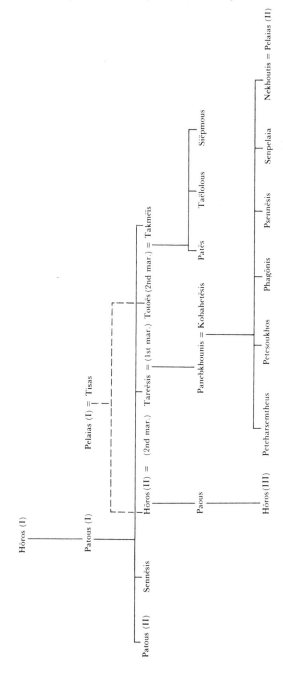

Fig. 6. Family tree of Peteharsemtheus son of Panebkhounis (immediate family only)

Egypt', as was Menkhes in Chapter 7. This family's surviving papers are, in the great majority, written in Greek, yet no person on the family tree ever appears under a Greek name. The likelihood, therefore, is that these people—unlike those of the three preceding families that we have studied—had no alternative Greek names, because they had no need of any. They were an Egyptian family living in an area populated almost entirely by Egyptians (as we saw in Chapter 6). But they continued to enjoy the status of Greeks that was conferred upon them hereditarily by a Greek or Macedonian ancestor in some earlier generation.

The Egyptians in the armed forces were a markedly privileged class, elevated far above the mass of their countrymen in status and attendant benefits. Those who opted for cleruchic status received allotments of land and housing, the others received rations and pay. We get the impression from the extant evidence that the men in both those categories generally made excellent use of their opportunities and prospered. That was certainly true of the family of Peteharsemtheus, which shows many signs of affluence. From the documents of his archive we learn that he and other members of his family owned buildings and parcels of land; they bought some, sold some, and gave some as gifts; and they engaged in numerous other business transactions.

Peteharsemtheus was the eldest son of the fifth and last generation recorded in the archive. While one or more of his brothers joined the army, he remained at home, conducting the family's affairs. He figures as a principal in just over half the extant documents; the rest of the papers belong or relate to earlier generations, especially the two generations immediately preceding his own.

Let us now take a closer look at the people in this family and their doings, as they are revealed by the contents of the archive. For the sake of clarity and convenience the numerals (I), (II), (III), will be used to assist in distinguishing individuals with the same name in different generations.

The earliest family member traceable is a man named Hōros, who was born sometime around 230 BC. This Horos (I) is the sole representative of his generation to appear in the archive, and at that he appears only as a patronym, that is, he is named as the father of Patous (I). We know nothing about his occupation or status. He would have been a youth when Egyptians were first enrolled in the army of the Ptolemies (see Chapter 1), and the family's hereditary privilege of military service could have begun with him. At all events, his son or sons surely enjoyed that privilege, as we deduce from the fact that two of his granddaughters married men of Greek military status.

Horos' son Patous was born, it would seem, sometime before 200 BC. As we can see that the family was reasonably prolific in the later generations for which the evidence is fuller, we may suppose that Patous had one or more siblings, but none appears in any of the documents of the archive. Patous himself had four children, a son (Patous II) and three daughters, the eldest born *c.*185 BC, the youngest in 164. Their father, Patous (I), was still alive at the end of 138 BC, when one of the documents records his borrowing 5,000 copper drachmas. When he died, not long after, that debt became the subject of a prolonged dispute, and it was finally discharged by two of his grandsons more than thirty years later.

It is in the third generation that this family really comes to life for us. Beginning then, and continuing for two generations thereafter, the documents of the archive parade several of the men and women of the family before us in glimpses of their private lives and, more often, of their business activities. It quickly becomes clear that this numerous family enjoyed a state of affluence that resided upon two firm bases, its military profession and its landholdings.

As we turn now to meet the members of the third generation, a new family enters our purview. Patous (I) had a contemporary named Pelaias who was, like himself, an Egyptian by name but in privilege and status 'a foreigner born in Egypt', that is, the native-born descendant of an immigrant to Ptolemaic Egypt. Pelaias and his wife Tisas had two sons (that is, two whom we know about; there may, of course, have been more). Those two sons were Totoēs (born *c.*183 BC), who ran the family estate, and Horos (II), who took up the career of professional soldier. The two brothers enter our picture because they married two daughters of Patous (I), the girls named Tareēsis and Takmeïs. They had an intertwined marital history, to wit:

1. Totoēs, when about eighteen years old, married Tareēsis, then about fifteen. In due course, in 163 BC, they had a son, Panebkhounis (who later became the father of Peteharsemtheus).

2. Sometime after 163 that marriage ended in divorce, and subsequently Tareēsis married her ex-husband's brother, Horos (II), by whom she had a son, Paous.

3. Totoēs, in turn, married Tareēsis' considerably younger sister, Takmeïs. The offspring of that marriage were a son and two daughters, born twenty and more years after Totoēs' son by his first marriage. More than idle curiosity would be served if we could know the events or considerations leading up to this second marriage. A similar difference in age marked the later nuptials of Dryton, in Chapter 6, when he married the young daughter of a fellow-soldier. No doubt Totoēs, even after his divorce from Tareēsis, still felt himself to be 'one of the family': not only did he have a son by his ex-wife, but she was now also his sister-in-law. And here was her younger sister blossoming into a handsome (if illiterate) adolescent, described to us in a much later document as being of medium height, olive-complexioned, flat-faced and straight-nosed. With Totoēs by her side they made an odd looking couple: he was short of stature, balding, olive-complexioned, with straight nose and hair (what there was of it), and a long face—no fashion plate, surely.[11] Furthermore, as he was approaching or perhaps already in middle age, he was old enough to be her father—in fact, she was only one year older than Panebkhounis, his son by his first marriage. On the other hand, he was a man of substance, a solid member of the community, a known quantity. A girl could do far worse—not that she was by any means a pauper, as we shall presently see. But let us look first at her husband's wealth.

The documents in which Totoēs figures as principal are five in number, and they are spread over a period of thirty-two years. The earliest, and the earliest of the whole archive, is a Demotic contract drawn up on 15 July 145 BC. It records that Totoēs, 'a foreigner born in Egypt', has paid 1,000 drachmas for a building lot located inside the fortifications of Pathyris; it is to be owned jointly by him and his brother, Horos (II), who is in the army. Some time thereafter they built a house on the lot, and some years after that Horos sold his share to Totoēs. The four other Totoēs documents are in Greek. One records a loan of 5,600 drachmas taken by Totoēs and his wife Takmēïs on 21 October 127 BC and repayable within three months. The other three documents were drawn up on 15 March 113 BC. On that day, as recorded on a papyrus now in the British Library, Totoēs borrowed from his son Panebkhounis the sum of 48,000 drachmas and thirteen artabs of wheat, all repayable a year and a half later, that is after the harvest of the following year, the second harvest to come. On that same 15 March Totoēs, now about seventy years old, made a division of properties which he owned among his two sons and two daughters, producing on that one day two separate documents with different provisions, an earlier and a later version, both of which are extant. The later one was final, and it was the one that took effect. Under both dispositions the daughters received less than half of what went to the sons, and under both Panebkhounis, the offspring of Totoēs' first marriage, received more than did his half-brother, Patēs. But in the first version, also preserved on a papyrus in the British Library, the favouritism shown the first-born was so glaring as to leave Patēs practically 'cut off with only a penny'. Abetted no doubt by his mother Takmēïs, he obviously waged a loud, swift, and successful campaign for more equitable treatment, for in the final disposition, preserved for us on a papyrus in Strasbourg, Panebkhounis' only advantage over Patēs is a half-share of the above-mentioned house in Pathyris, in which Patēs does not share at all. Here, in summary, are Totoēs' final dispositions: of a three-aroura landholding, one aroura goes to each son, a half-aroura to each daughter; another holding, measuring six and two-thirds arouras, is divided in the same proportions; a building lot is divided equally between the sons; and ownership of the house within the fortifications goes one-half to Panebkhounis and one-quarter to each of the daughters. Nine months later, with their father's approval, the two daughters sold their half of the house to Panebkhounis' wife.[12]

Let us turn now to Totoēs' second wife, Takmēïs (or

Takmēous, as the name appears once, apparently a variant with a suffix of endearment). As already mentioned, she was no child of poverty when Totoēs married her. She doubtless brought him a sizeable dowry, but as the documents reveal, she also retained certain properties in her own right and was able to dispose of them at will. She appears as principal in five documents of the archive. The earliest, with a date corresponding to 1 February 136 BC, records that she lent her brother Patous (II) an iron cone (presumably an agricultural implement) worth 8,000 copper drachmas. On 5 November 136 she and Patous sold, for 10,000 drachmas, a sycamore tree that they owned jointly, and she then made him a loan, repayable after the next harvest, of her half of the proceeds of the sale. The high price which they received for the tree reminds us, incidentally, of how scarce wood was, and is, in Egypt's dry climate and soil. Next in time comes the already cited document of 127 BC by which Totoēs and Takmēïs jointly contracted a debt of 5,600 drachmas. About a year after that Takmēïs gave three parcels of land to her three children. Eleven years later, on 7 April 114, the children deeded the parcels back to her, and soon after, on 3 September, the parcels were sold for 8,000 drachmas to Peteharsemtheus, Takmēïs and one daughter being named as the sellers and stated to be acting with the consent of the other daughter and her half-brother (who was the father of the buyer). There is, surprisingly (to us at least), no mention of the full brother, who, as we know from other documents, was not deceased. As to why he was ignored, at least in the writing, we can only speculate, but it may be relevant to recall the unequal treatment he received in his father's will of the following year.

The next member of the family to claim our attention is that half-brother, Panebkhounis, or Panobkhounis (the name is written both ways in Greek; the Demotic omits the final -is). No doubt because he was the father of Peteharsemtheus, the keeper of this family archive, he figures more prominently in these papers than any family member we have yet encountered. He was born in 163 BC, and *c.*140 he married Kobahetēsis (her name also omits the final -is in Demotic), who was then only thirteen years old, ten years or so younger than himself. She was also known by another name, Maithōtis. But, unlike the dual names in our previously studied families, neither of her names contains any Greek element; both are purely Egyptian —a further indication of how completely Egyptian the lifestyle of the privileged families of this milieu had become, even though they continued to enjoy the hereditary status of 'Greeks born in Egypt'.

In middle age Panebkhounis was, according to one of the documents, of medium height (his mother's genes there, his father having been short), olive-complexioned, round-faced, with straight nose and hair that was receding in front, and a scar at the right-hand peak of his bald patch. His wife is described (in another document) as being short to medium in height, olive-complexioned, with round face and straight nose. Their marriage produced, over a period of some twenty-five years, four sons and two daughters who survived to adulthood; there were likely to have been, in between, other offspring who died in infancy or early childhood, but there is no occasion for them to be mentioned in the documents of the archive. Panebkhounis lived until some time after 99 BC; his wife survived him, but we do not know for how long.

Panebkhounis was the man of his generation who carried on the traditional family career of professional soldier. Like others of that status whom we encountered earlier, he was not prevented by his garrison duties from continuing to see to his lands and other business interests. He figures in some twenty documents, which range in date from 131 to 99 BC. Eight of the documents, four Greek and four Demotic, are receipts for tax payments that he made between the years 131 and 102. Two of them record payments in wheat, one by himself and the other jointly with his brother, from the crops of his fields planted to cereals. Four are payments of amounts from 720 to 2,200 drachmas for the use of pasture land belonging to the crown. There is also a payment of 200 drachmas for the sales tax of 10 per cent on four plots of land that he bought in 115 BC, and a 1,600 drachma payment for the 10 per cent levy on vine land.[14]

Although these tax receipts are clear enough evidence of some of his agricultural activities, the light which they shed is indirect and indistinct. Eight other papyri provide actual records of some of Panebkhounis' business transactions. Mention has already been made of the loan of 48,000 drachmas and thirteen artabs of wheat that he made to his father, Totoēs, on 15 March 113 BC. A Demotic document of 6 March 125 BC is an agreement by another professional soldier, who was about to build an adjacent house, not to block Panebkhounis' lightwell or even have a window on that side of his new house. On 19 November 123 we see Panebkhounis and his wife buying from her brother, for 4,000 drachmas, one-quarter aroura of land along the Nile. On 10 September 112 he borrowed 7,000 drachmas, giving as security a small piece of land, which was returned to him when he repaid the loan a year later. On 24 February 107 he bought half a house for 12,000 drachmas and paid the 10 per cent sales tax at Krokodilopolis. As he and his wife already owned a house together in nearby Pathyris, this purchase may have been intended to provide them with a residence on those occasions when he was assigned to military duty at Krokodilopolis; or, of course, the house may have been bought as an investment. Six weeks earlier, on 12 January, Panebkhounis and his eldest son, Peteharsemtheus, were signatories to an extraordinary document, one of the most important in the whole archive for what it tells us not only about contemporary law but also about the sense of collective responsibility—a veritable code of *noblesse oblige*—that characterized, in all likelihood, not this family alone but the whole privileged class of Egyptian soldiery enjoying Greek status. The document of 12 January 107 records the payment of 8,100 drachmas by Peteharsemtheus and his father to a certain Chairēmōn (Greek) also known as Herienoupis (Egyptian), the son of a professional soldier stationed at Krokodilopolis. The 8,100 drachmas comprised 4,500 owed by Panebkhounis himself and 3,600 being paid on behalf of his aunt Sennēsis, part of a larger sum which she had borrowed from Chairemon's father-in-law thirty-one years ago, in the year 138! The 5,000 drachmas still due on that long overdue debt were paid off—with Chairemon waiving the penalties for delinquency or tardiness—on 20 April 104, more than three years later, apparently (see below) with money obtained by taking a loan from Horos (III), a half-cousin of Peteharsemtheus.[15]

There remain two important documents concerning Paneb-khounis still to be considered. One is in Demotic, the other in Greek. The latter tells us about the purchase, sale, and repurchase of the same parcels of land, and the dates of those transactions strongly suggest that the sale and repurchase were coloured by the circumstances indicated in the earlier Demotic document. If so, we are treated to an unusually intimate glimpse of a story of timeless human interest.

Let us begin, then, with the Demotic document, drawn up some time in the year 105/4 BC. In it Peteharsemtheus and his three brothers recorded their agreement on three matters: first, how they would share their paternal estate when the time came; secondly, that they would jointly provide for their father's maintenance for the rest of his life; and thirdly, that after his death they would continue to provide for their mother as long as she lived. Obviously, there is more here than meets the eye, but we can only speculate about the underlying circumstances, on which the document is absolutely (and discreetly?) silent. Panebkhounis, the father of the signatories, was then fifty-eight years old, well beyond the average life span of ancient times. Had he been stricken by what looked like a terminal illness? If so, he recovered, or at the very least continued in life for some few more years, as we shall see in a moment. Or, had he begun to show signs of erratic behaviour which his alarmed sons thought might diminish the family fortune? Some such possibility is suggested by the Greek document, which was drawn up in 99 BC. It tells us on 30 December 115, Panebkhounis had bought four parcels of land, price not stated. He owned, and presumably farmed, that land for fifteen and a half years, until 6 June 99, when he sold the four parcels for 12,000 drachmas. We note that the sale took place some five or six years after the maintenance agreement entered into by his sons. Panebkhounis was evidently still alive. But his action in selling the four parcels clearly did not meet with his sons' approval, for less than eight weeks later Peteharsemetheus bought the parcels back—and at no increase in price, which strongly suggests a mutual recognition by the parties that Panebkhounis' sale of a few weeks back would not withstand a legal challenge.[16]

Meanwhile, what of Kobahetēsis, Panebkhounis' wife? We

have already recorded that she was ten years younger than her husband, that she presumably survived him, and that the couple owned some properties jointly. It remains only to add that in her married years she occasionally acquired property either in her own name alone or jointly with her sons. Beyond that, she is little more than a name to us.

A detail that deserves mention here in passing is the rather casual attitude of those days toward the specification of an individual's age, which was a standard element in the identification of the parties to a legal instrument such as a contract. In the house purchase of 107 BC, Panebkhounis' age is given as 'about sixty'; he was then fifty-five or fifty-six. In the document of 99 BC described above, eight and a half years later, he is still 'about sixty'. Even more striking is the description of Panebkhounis' father, Totoēs, as 'about fifty-five' at a time when he was some fifteen years older than that; being married to a much younger wife must have kept him younger-looking.[17]

We turn now to the fifth generation, in which the leading figure is Peteharsemtheus, the eldest son of Panebkhounis and Kobahetēsis. After him were born three more sons—Petesoukhos, Phagōnis (named after his mother's father), and Psennēsis—and two daughters, Senpelaia and Nekhoutis. Peteharsemtheus managed the family's estates and business affairs. It was the second son, Petesoukhos, who pursued the hereditary military career, and his younger sister married such a military man—a man, in other words, from their own privileged milieu. Their marriage contract of 3 March 99 BC is found in the archive, and it again forcefully reminds us that these were Egyptian families whose lives conformed to the traditional ways of the native culture: the bridegroom enjoyed the inherited status of 'a Greek born in Egypt', the bride was the daughter of such another, but the marriage contract is written in Demotic. The text of the contract is given at the end of this chapter.

Peteharsemtheus is the principal figure, acting sometimes alone and sometimes in concert with one or more of his brothers, in some three dozen papyri dating from 114 to 88 BC or possibly later. Twelve of the papyri contain contracts or receipts relating to loans. Five are tax receipts, all of these in

Demotic. Fourteen of the documents are sales or purchases of land, two of them having the effect of keeping property in the family, even though under a new owner. Thus, on 3 September 114 BC Peteharsemtheus bought three parcels of land from Takmeïs and her daughter Siëpmous, who was a half-sister of his father. Takmeïs' husband, Totoës, was still alive at a fairly advanced age, and he appears in the document as the legal representative of his wife and daughter. Another daughter, Taëlolous, and her half-brother, Peteharsemtheus' father, renounce whatever rights they may have had in the property. Here is the text of that contract of sale.

[Date.] In Pathyris, before Ammonios, keeper of records. Takmeïs daughter of Patous . . . about 50 years old, of medium height, olive-complexioned, flat-faced, straight-nosed, and Siëpmous daughter of Totoës . . . about 25 years old, of medium height, dark-complexioned, long-faced, straight-nosed, with the husband of Takmeïs and father of Siëpmous—viz. Totoës son of Pelaias—as their legal representative, and with the consent of Panobkhounis [*sic*] and Taëlolous, children of Totoës, have sold the share belonging to each of them of three parcels of grain-bearing river-bank land in Pathyris. Boundaries of Parcel 1: south, land of Pakhratēs and Koulis, north, land of Khens-thōtēs, east, land of Aēs, west, a dike, [next, the boundaries of Parcels 2 and 3 similarly stated, the eastern side of 3 running along the Nile]—or whoever the adjoiners may be everywhere. It was purchased by Peteharsemtheus son of Panobkhounis for 1 talent 2,000 drachmas in copper. Guarantors are Takmeïs and Siëpmous, the sellers, whom Peteharsemtheus, the buyer, accepted [as guarantors].
   I, Ammonios, have registered it.
[10 Sept.] Paid into the Pathyris bank headed by Hera/ the one-tenth assessment of sales tax, by Peteharsemtheus son of Panob-khounis, copper 800 (total, 800).
         [Signed] Hera/ ban/[18]

A year later, on 27 August 113 BC, Peteharsemtheus' maternal grandmother sold a small strip of land, the buyers being Peteharsemtheus for a two-fifths share and, for the other three-fifths, Taëlolous, to whom, as we have just been reminded, he was related through his father.[19]

The rest of the purchases were made from outside the family. For example, on 15 November 107 Peteharsemtheus and his three brothers bought three and a half arouras for

54,000 drachmas, a somewhat higher-than-average price, no
doubt owing to the parcel's favourable location by the river.[20]

Deserving specific mention, finally, are some of the documents recording loans made or taken. On 10 December 103
Peteharsemtheus and his three brothers repaid a loan they
had taken from their half-cousin Horos (III) and his father;
from the description of the loan it looks as though the amount,
not stated, was the 5,000 drachmas needed the year before to
extinguish the balance of the longstanding debt of their great-
aunt Sennesis (p. 147). Three other loans also have more than
routine interest, one of them taken by Peteharsemtheus alone,
the other two jointly with Petesoukhos, his soldier-brother, one
of them on that same 10 December 103, the other two either
about that time or within the ensuing nine months. On 10
December the brothers, owing 11,200 drachmas, paid back all
but 5,100 of the total and signed a new note for the
outstanding amount, which they obviously used to pay off
their half-cousin Horos (III) on that day. The other two loans
are for 12,000 and 18,000 drachmas, respectively. As we know
that this was a propertied family in easy circumstances, it is
not likely that those substantial loans were taken to meet any
pressing need; rather they may be seen as constituting
additional capital on which they expected to show a profit, in
some agricultural or other business enterprise. In that
connection we observe, too, that on 11 December, the very
day after he incurred a debt of 5,100 drachmas, Peteharsemtheus acquired through foreclosure a piece of land on which he
held a mortgage of 11,500 drachmas.[21]

As our parting glance at this prolific and affluent family of
the local military gentry, here is the marriage contract of its
youngest member known to us, Nekhoutis, Peteharsemtheus'
youngest sister. It was written in Demotic on the day
corresponding to 3 March 99 BC.

Regnal year 15, month 2 of the winter season, day 18, of Pharaoh
Ptolemy [X] who is called Alexandros and of his Queen Berenikē,
his sister, his wife [and the rest of the elaborate opening formula: see
above, note 7].
The Greek born in Egypt, Pelaias (II) son of Bias and Isarion has
said to the woman Nekhoutis daughter of Panebkhoun and Kobahetēs:
I have made you my wife.

I have given you 100 silver pieces (= 500 staters, which, again, = 100 silver pieces) and 10 artabs of wheat (half = wheat 5, total = 10 artabs of wheat) as your wife-gift.

Your eldest son, my eldest son, amongst the children you will bear me is lord of each and every thing I now possess and will hereafter acquire.

Here is an itemized list of your feminine gear that you have brought with your own hand into my house:

one veil[?]	worth 230 silver pieces
one garment	worth 200 silver pieces
one jar	worth 200 silver pieces
two necklaces	worth 150 silver pieces
three arm-rings	worth 200 silver pieces
three other arm-rings	worth 100 silver pieces
one sieve	worth 100 silver pieces
one brazier	worth 100 silver pieces

[etc. to a total of some thousands of silver pieces].[22]

Epilogue

When, in 301 BC, the Macedonian generals competing to succeed Alexander the Great settled down in their three Hellenistic kingdoms, it was as if a floodgate had been opened in the Greek world. From its city-states, devastated and impoverished by a hundred years and more of incessant wars, waves of humanity—men, women, whole families—poured into the ancient oriental lands of the Near East, now lands of opportunity for them. The chief of those lodestones it seems, affording the greatest opportunities, was Egypt, which would be ruled for close to 300 years thereafter by Ptolemy son of Lagos and his descendants. And the thousands of papyri of Ptolemaic date unearthed in Egypt in the past hundred years give us a picture of life there which, in its detailed intimacy and immediacy, is without parallel for any other area of the Hellenistic world.

The immigrant flood from the Greek-speaking world continued in full spate for decades before tapering off to trickles. In the earlier chapters of this book, set in the third century BC, we encountered representative members of that immigrant population. In government service, military and civilian, and in various commercial activities they prospered —most of them—in their adopted homeland. They all had Greek names and patronyms, proud symbols of their ancestry, the basis of their present privileged status. Their language, too, remained exclusively Greek, as we see in the surviving documents. With the classic attitude of an imperial ruling class, they left the attainment of bilingual ability almost entirely to those members of the Egyptian underclass who were ambitious to get ahead.

In the chapters that make up the second half of this book, in similar settings of a hundred years later, the protagonists bear dual names, Egyptian as well as Greek, and finally Egyptian names alone, and documents written in the native tongue appear with increasing frequency. What is more, men with such outlandish (to Greeks) Egyptian names as Panebkhoun and Menkhes are actually styled 'Greeks [or 'foreigners'] born in Egypt'. Is this not clear evidence that a fusion of the two cultures had indeed taken place?

For over a hundred years, until quite recently, scholars thought the answer to that question was yes, and there would have been no reason to reverse that opinion if the men and women of Chapter 6–8 were typical of the Egyptian population as a whole under Ptolemaic rule. But we now know, thanks to the accumulated evidence of the papyri, that Menkhes and Peteharsemtheus and the others who people the last chapters were, in truth, members of a small élite of native Egyptians, a privileged minority which their families, in varying degrees bilingual, had entered as the result of an intermarriage with some man of Greek or Macedonian descent somewhere along the line. These more or less Hellenized Egyptians are prominent in the civil and military services, mostly in the lower ranks, but with the passing decades a few of them even rose to army generalships and other top-level offices, such as those of strategos and epistrategos. But even those rare individuals, although exalted by their high office to such honorific titles as 'king's cousin', never claimed to be Greeks, let alone those in the lower echelons such as Menkhes and Panebkhounis and their kind; and no one, least of all they themselves, ever thought of them as anything other than Egyptians. The designation 'Greeks born in Egypt' was an ingenious legalistic straddle, affirming their right, though they were not ethnic Greeks, to enjoy the privileged status they inherited from a forebear of Greek or Macedonian ancestry.

Ptolemaic Egypt, in other words, remained throughout its history a land of two cultures which did coexist but, for the most part, did not coalesce or blend. The families of Greek and Macedonian ancestry, proud of being a 'master race', saw to that. We who study the history of those times, a history now so richly documented by the archaeological finds of the past hundred years, discern the manifestations of the two discrete cultures in every aspect of their coexistence. The following is a particularly striking illustration. In ordinary cultural contacts handy words in the language of one group are readily adopted into the language of the other group. It would be difficult, therefore, to exaggerate the significance of the fact that, except for some local designations of places, measures, and so on, no native Egyptian word made its way into Greek usage in the thousand years that Greek endured as the language of Ptolemaic, Roman, and Byzantine Egypt. That phenomenon can only mean that the Greek-speaking population actively resisted using or adopting Egyptian parlance. In fact, when a need arose they would exhume and resurrect a Greek term fallen into desuetude rather than introduce the available Egyptian word into their language and usage.

In the spring of 47 BC Kleopatra VII Thea Philopator, the last ruler of the Ptolemaic dynasty, set out with her Roman paramour, Julius Caesar, on a leisurely Nile cruise. Thus she would while away the final months of her now very visible pregnancy, while displaying to him the archaeological and economic riches of the realm she now ruled by his grace. Accompanied by a flotilla of 400 vessels carrying servants, supplies, and (Roman) soldiers, the couple disported themselves on a royal houseboat of enormous size and incredibly luxurious in its appointments. Even allowing for exaggeration in its description by the anecdotist Athenaios (second/third century AD), we must still picture a leviathan of a vessel, propelled by several banks of oarsmen; it was fitted out with—in addition to bedrooms and salons—colonnaded courts, banquet halls, a winter garden, shrines of Aphrodite and Dionysos (love and wine—what more appropriate?); and decorated with lavish employment of cedar and cypress woods, varied paints, and gold leaf.[1]

As they moved up the Nile, the two cultures of Hellenistic Egypt were paraded before their eyes. The setting from which they began their journey was purely Greek, the royal palace in Alexandria and hard by it the famous museum and library, for the past two and a half centuries the world's leading centre of Greek scholarship in the arts and sciences. There were, of course, non-Greeks too in the melting pot that was Alexandria. The Egyptian language was still spoken in the native quarters there, and the harbourside rang with the babel of many foreign tongues. But all the main business of Alexandria, not only its government and its intellectual life, not only its domestic enterprises, but even its far-flung commerce, was conducted in Greek.

As the royal houseboat pursued its leisurely course upstream (and again on its downstream return), throngs of people from nearby towns and villages would line the river banks to glimpse and acclaim their sovereign and her conquering hero. Detachments of military from the local garrisons and settlements would be posted along the way to contain the crowds and assure the safety of the royal party, as well as to add their own voices to the huzzahs. In the early stages of the royal progress the soldiers would mostly be shouting their cheers in Greek, but the farther the party proceeded upstream the less frequent Greek would become and the more the native tongue would be heard. Six hundred kilometres from Alexandria they would pass almost the last of the Greek outposts, the city of Ptolemais, and the garrison town of Little Diospolis on the approaches to Thebes. A little way beyond Thebes lay Egyptian Pathyris, home of the families of Dryton and Peteharsemtheus. At Thebes itself, since the dawn of history the headquarters of the most powerful of the Egyptian priesthoods, the high priest with an appropriate retinue doubtless waited at the landing-stage, as he was in duty bound to do, to greet his queen. There the queen no doubt showed them the courtesy of conversing with them in their native tongue. The last of the Ptolemies, we are told by Plutarch, was the first of the Ptolemies to learn to speak Egyptian.[2]

Glossary

aroura: literally 'plough land', the term used in Ptolemaic Egypt as the standard unit of land area, equivalent to 0.68 acres, or 0.275 hectares.

artab: Anglicized spelling of Greek *artabē*, the principal unit of dry measure, used for grains and other produce. While the unit capacity varied considerably with time and place, the most common artab was apparently the one equivalent to approximately 1⅙ bushels, or 43 litres. A recent discussion of the complex ancient evidence appeared in *Zeitschrift für Papyrologie und Epigraphik*, 42 (1981), 101. In the form *ardib*, or *irdib*, the term still survives in Egyptian usage.

cleruch: Anglicized spelling of Greek *klērouchos*, 'allotment holder', the technical designation of a man rewarded with an allotment of land (*klēros*) and housing in return for his enrolment as a military reservist. The status of cleruch quickly became hereditary from father to son. Enrolment was opened to native Egyptians late in the third century BC.

Demotic ('popular'): the term by which modern scholarship designates the cursive script in which the Egyptian language was written from the sixth century BC to the fourth century AD.

drachma: the basic currency unit of the Greek world, varying in weight in different places. Most widely used was the Athenian standard, in which a silver four-drachma piece, or a tetradrachm, weighed approximately seventeen grams. In the prices prevailing at the end of 1985 that weight of silver was worth about £2,20p, or $3.25.

king's cousin: an honorary title awarded almost automatically to members of the king's court and to men who attained high office, such as that of strategos, in the royal administration.

klēros: see *cleruch*.

nome: Anglicized spelling of Greek *nomos* (plural *nomoi*), the Ptolemaic term for the three dozen or so administrative districts of Egypt, each headed by a strategos (q.v.).

obol: one-sixth of a drachma.

papyrus: the name of an aquatic plant *Cyperus papyrus*, L.), and of the writing paper made from it in Egypt and used throughout the ancient world.

strategos: the governor of a nome, the king's representative in charge of the military forces there as well as of the civil and judicial administration.

talent: a unit of monetary reckoning, equal to 60,000 drachmas.

toparchy: a division of a nome (q.v.).

Notes

INTRODUCTION

1. *Journal of Egyptian Archaeology*, 6 (1920), 161.
2. Isokrates' exhortation to the Greek cities to combine against Persia is the subject of his *Panegyrikos*. The plea to the Macedonian king is found in his *Philippos* (346 BC) and in two letters written in 344 and 338. In the standard editions of the orator's works those are, respectively, Orations IV and V, and Letters II and III. The authenticity of this last has been much debated.
3. *Inter alia*, much weight used to be placed on the appearance in the documents of men and women, offspring of mixed marriages, who bore double names, one Greek the other Egyptian. But it is now clear that they were but a small minority of the population, individuals to be found, usually, in special situations such as those illustrated in Chapters 6–8 of this book. As summed up by J. Mélèze-Modrzejewski (*Revue des études grecques*, 96 [1983], 248), 'In any case, one thing remains certain: Ptolemaic onomastics can today no longer serve as a support—as it used to at the beginning of this century—for syncretistic theories postulating a "mixture of the races" and a "fusion of the civilizations".'
4. But old notions die hard. In a lecture delivered on 6 March 1973 by H. S. Smith we still find the statement that 'the ancient culture . . . of the Kingdoms of the Near East became inextricably fused with the polity and civilization of the Greek world. This fused Hellenistic culture . . .' (*A Visit to Ancient Egypt* [Warminster, 1974], 2). *Contra*, J. Mélèze-Modrzejewski, loc. cit., 254: 'The idea of a "barbarization" of the Greek element, drowned in the Egyptian milieu to the point of being "dead" by the time of the Roman conquest of Egypt, is probably as fallacious as that of the "Hellenization" of the Orient, [an idea] which was current in the '20s but is seen today as a product for the most part of a certain colonial ideology in Western historiography of those times.'
5. Ibid. 255: 'In sum, fusion extended only to limited groups—"fringes of copenetration", as Edouard Will calls them [in *Ancient Society*, 1979]—on the one hand Hellenized native élites, on the other hand certain Greeks absorbed into the local milieu. The importance of these fringes for the study of the colonial society of Hellenistic Egypt is considerable; they nevertheless constitute a marginal phenomenon of that society . . . These [military men of Chapters 6 and 8] do not reflect Ptolemaic society as a whole. The postulate of "fusion" rests in fact on the fragile base of a special phenomenon of limited scope.'
6. The duality of the Ptolemaic kingship is revealed by many elements in the sources, of which the following is surely the most piquant. One of

the prime clues that led Champollion to the decipherment of the hieroglyphics was the Egyptian practice of enclosing a Pharaoh's name in a cartouche. In documents of Ptolemaic date written in the Egyptian language, the king's name is indeed treated as that of a Pharaoh by being enclosed in a cartouche—but only in some instances; in others the cartouche is omitted and the royal name is followed by the sign for 'of the foreign people'.

The abuses with which local officials are charged in extant documents include extortion, the taking of bribes and 'protection' money, torture, and physical violence (often with whips, knives, and cudgels). These were, of course, breaches of publicly proclaimed policies of the royal administration, which enjoined its functionaries to earn deserved popularity by displaying, in the discharge of their duties, such virtues as concern for everybody and everything, diligence, good will, forethought, effort, attention, sobriety, zeal, respect, assiduity, protection, precision, vigilance—all with a view to assuring 'that people are treated justly' (*UPZ* 111). *P. Teb.* 703, of *c.*240–210 BC, a long list of specific instructions from the finance minister to his operatives in the nomes, concludes with this general advice: 'Your guiding principle must be to proceed personally, honestly and according to the highest good . . . secondly, to behave correctly and uprightly in your district, not get involved with bad company, avoid all collusion toward evil purposes, and consider that if you are irreproachable in these regards you will be deemed worthy of higher office' (lines 261–77). A typical case of official abuse—to cite but one of dozens—is revealed in this letter of 156 BC from the then finance minister to an official in the Memphite nome (*P. Par.* 61R = *UPZ* 113):

> Whereas the king and queen consider it important that all under their rule be treated justly; and whereas not a few people have come down to Alexandria to complain against you, or those under you, or—most especially—the tax farmers, charging them with fraudulent exactions and extortions, and some even alleging that they are being blackmailed;
>
> We therefore want you to be quite clear that all such acts are foreign to our administration, as it will be to your tenure of office if any of the personnel referred to is proved to have injured anyone. Therefore, in order that nothing of the sort may occur again, that no one be treated unjustly by anyone (and especially by tax farmers trying blackmail), you are, as a matter of urgency, to be on guard yourself and are also to send orders to those referred to about the said offences.

7. There are excellent accounts of the revolts by C. Préaux in *Chronique d' Égypte*, 11 (1936) and 40 (1965). In a more recent treatment of the subject W. Peremans discerns the revolts as stemming more from social than from nationalistic causes (in H. Maehler and V. M. Strocka, eds., *Das ptolemäische Aegypten* [Mainz, 1978], 39–50.

8. J. Mélèze-Modrzejewski, loc. cit., 242–3.

CHAPTER I

1. The occurrences in the *Odyssey* are at Book 3, verses 300–2, 4. 126–7 and 228–32, and 14. 285–6 for the first four; the other two are 14. 246–84 and 17. 425–44. For the history of the Peoples of the Sea one may now consult the new edition of the *Cambridge Ancient History*, Volume II, Part 2 (1975), esp. 366–71; other bibliography will be found in the index there, p. 1106.

2. Herondas, *Mimes* 1. 23–6. The 'sibling gods' were Ptolemy II and his sister-wife Arsinoë; see further p. 165 below.

3. Theokritos, *Idylls* 14. 58–68.

4. The ancient evidence and modern bibliography on the Pharos are detailed in P. M. Fraser, *Ptolemaic Alexandria* (Oxford, 1972), Volume II, notes 96–117 (pp. 43–52). The wording of the dedicatory inscription is preserved for us in Section 62 of the essay *How to Write History* by the second-century satirist Lucian. A glass vase in the shape of the Pharos, found in Afghanistan, is a particularly dramatic reminder of the far-flung fame of Alexandria's lighthouse.

5. *P. Mich. Zenon* 10. On routes and conditions of travel see L. Casson, *Travel in the Ancient World* (London, 1974), *passim*.

6. Ibid., 157 and 161–2. The second quotation translates a writer of the fifth century AD, but neither the climate nor the modalities of shipping in the Mediterranean had changed by then from what they were in Hellenistic times.

7. *P. Cairo Zenon* 59021 is the letter quoted at the beginning of the paragraph. Examples of the importation of slaves, horses, and other animals: as gifts for the king from a 'sheikh' in Transjordan, *P. Cairo Zenon* 59075 and 59076 = *Corpus Papyrorum Judaicarum* 5 and 4. Other slaves: *P. Cairo Zenon* 59093. All three documents date from 257 BC.

8. *P. Lond.* 2026.

9. The complaint of the wine sellers is found in *P. Ent.* 34. A concessionaire of the oil monopoly appears on p. 119.

10. Shipowners in 'the uppermost layers of Ptolemaic society' are listed by H. Hauben, *Ancient Society*, 10 (1979), 168. Kleopatra appears in *SB* 11866, datable to *c.*150–100 BC. Vessels carrying 200 artabs are encountered in several documents, e.g. *P. Ryl.* 576, the 'supertanker' of 10,000 artabs' burthen in *P. Ent.* 27. The different types of vessel and their capacities are detailed in L. Casson, *Ships and Seamanship in the Ancient World* (Princeton, 1971), 333–5 and 340–3.

11. *P. Par.* 62 = *UPZ* 112. In addition to all the 'red tape' apparent in these regulations, tax farmers often had to cope with delays caused by local officials who were less than co-operative in making needed records available in good time; an example of this appears on p. 51.

    The 'intercalary days', mentioned in the opening sentence of the text, are explained in the Prefatory Notes.

12. The activity of the middlemen was discerned by J. Bingen: see his papers in *Illinois Classical Studies*, 3 (1978), 74–8, and in *Problèmes de la terre . . .* , ed. M. I. Finley (The Hague, 1973), 215–22.

13. Greek mercenaries were far from a new phenomenon in Egypt, where they had been employed by the Pharaohs since the seventh century BC (above, p. 9). Athens had sent soldiers to help Egypt against Persia in 459–456 BC, and for most of the fourth century, until eleven years before Alexander's conquest, the Pharaohs depended upon Greek mercenaries to help them maintain a precarious independence constantly threatened by Persia.

14. On the development of hereditary rights in the military, see further below, pp. 24 and 33–4. When the settler-reservists were mobilized, the élite corps, such as the cavalry, went to battle in style, as we observe in the following complaint submitted in 217 BC to the strategos of the Arsinoite nome:

> I, Pistos of Leontomenēs, am wronged by Aristokratēs, Thracian, 100-aroura holder, of the first cavalry division, a colonist in [the village of] Autodikē. [Six months ago] I hired myself out to him by written contract . . . to be his squire on the campaign [against Syria] and render him my services till I saw him safely back in Autodikē, receiving from him as a monthly wage the amount agreed upon between us. I have rendered him my services and behaved irreproachably and seen him safely back to Autodikē, as the contract provides, but Aristokrates still owes me ten drachmas of my wages, and though I keep asking for it he does not pay up.

See notes 16 and 18, below, and Chapter 4 for further examples of this complaint procedure.

In the third century BC Jewish immigrants to Egypt, in contrast to the later military settlers, were principally professional and business men, skilled workers, and scholars, who took up residence, for the most part, in and near Alexandria. It was there in the mid-third century that the Septuagint, the Greek translation of the Hebrew Bible, was produced.

15. The documents are *P. Petrie* III 20 = *W. Chr.* 450 = *Select Papyri* 413 = *C. Ord. Ptol.* 5–10. See also the comments of M. Th. Lenger in *Chronique d'Égypte*, 27 (1952), 218–46 and 29 (1954), 124–36.

16. The two documents quoted are *P. Lond.* 106 = *UPZ* 151, and *P. Hal.* 1, lines 166–79 = *Select Papyri* 207. Another example of such abuses appears on p. 60. In petitions the address to the king—the 'shepherd of his flock'—was purely a formality, the complaint being submitted in actuality to the nome strategos: see further in Chapter 4.

17. *P. Ent.* 11 = *W. Chr.* 449.

18. *P. Ent.* 13.

19. *P. Lond.* 2027. As the editor, T. C. Skeat, remarks in his introduction to that document, 'The writer must have been a person of some standing.' Otherwise, for one thing, the proper etiquette would have required that he place his name after Zenon's in the salutation, i.e., 'To Zenon greeting from Asklepiades'.

20. The data are found in *P. Teb.* I 60–2 and p. 538. The royal, or crown, land was cultivated by 'crown farmers', i.e. tenant farmers who contracted for the several fields and plots with the appropriate local

officials of the royal administration. Cleruchic land was, in large part, similarly contracted out for cultivation by local peasants: see pp. 20 and 32.

21. R. S. Bagnall, *The Administration of the Ptolemaic Possessions outside Egypt* (Leiden, 1976), 238. It is not until the year 1 BC, by which time Egypt had been a province of the Roman Empire for three decades, that there appears in the documents a member of a village gymnasium who, while his own name is Greek, has a father whose name is Egyptian: Antaios son of Onnōphris (*BGU* 1189). Whether Boïdas son of Demetrios, who appears as gymnasiarch and kosmētēs in an inscription of the second or first century BC (*SEG* XX 672 = *SB* 7246), was an Egyptian, as has been claimed by some scholars, is problematical.

22. In *Ancient Society*, 5 (1974), 135, W. Peremans points out that of the 133 by then recorded families in which fathers with Egyptian names had sons with Greek names, sixty-four (or just under half) were families engaged in agriculture or cattle raising; and that only one-eighth of those sixty-four occurred in the third century BC, the other seven-eighths in the second and first centuries. Peremans concludes: 'In sum, we are entitled to believe that the rapprochement between indigenes and immigrants occurred primarily in the popular classes and that [in that milieu] Egyptianization prevailed over Hellenization.'

The example of 250 BC is found in *P. Cairo Zenon* 59292, lines 300–1.

23. *P. Par.* 13 = *UPZ* 123.

24. 'The evolution of the Ptolemaic nobility, and therefore of the Ptolemaic state, can further be demonstrated by the appearance, from the end of the second century, of some Egyptian families in the upper strata of officialdom. Their road had been long and arduous.' (L. Mooren, *Proc. Sixteenth International Congr. Papyrology* [*Amer. Stud. in Papyrology* 23, 1981], 301.) For examples see id., *The Aulic Titulature* (Brussels, 1975), and *Zeitschrift für Papyrologie und Epigraphik*, 27 (1977), 190–1 (an especially interesting case of three generations of the same family); also W. Clarysse, *Ancient Society*, 7 (1976), 185–207. Most interesting of all, probably, is the Paōs who appears in *UPZ* 209 of 129 BC. He was epistrategos and strategos of the Thebaid, which (if he had not received it before) entitled him to the honorific appellative of 'king's cousin', and he had a Greek deputy! (*UPZ* 215, of 130 BC).

25. Writing in 1977 (*Ancient Society*, 8, 181–2), W. Peremans was able to cite only six military officers, all in documents of the second and first centuries, who clearly or probably belonged to mixed Graeco-Egyptian families.

26. The 500 'Cretans' appear in *P. Teb.* 32, lines 16–17. On the *politeumata* in general see D. J. Thompson (Crawford), *Atti XVII Congr. Int. Papirologia* (Naples, 1984), 1069–75.

27. The document is *P. Teb.* 62. See the detailed discussion by D. J. (Thompson) Crawford, *Kerkeosiris, an Egyptian Village in the Ptolemaic Period* (Cambridge, 1971), 103. The 'present king' referred to in the text was Ptolemy VIII, who ruled from 145 to 116 BC; his brother was Ptolemy VI, 180–145, his father Ptolemy V, 204–180, his grandfather Ptolemy IV, 221–204.

28. Examples or mentions of leases from the third century are *BGU* 1943, 1944, 1958, 1959; *P. Ent.* 52, 54, 55, 59; *P. Petrie* III 104–6; *P. Sorb.* 14 and the parallel texts cited there. On the whole matter, see also the references in note 12, above.

29. The quotation is from *P. Lille* 4 = *W. Chr.* 336, lines 30–3. The orphans appear in *P. Petrie* II 39(e) = III 110(a) 1; the whole question of the orphans has recently been reviewed by L. Criscuolo, *Proc. Sixteenth International Congr. Papyrology* [*Amer. Stud. in Papyrology* 23, 1981], 259–65. In *P. Lille* 14 = *W. Chr.* 335, of 242 BC, the state actually takes back a *klēros* from its holder and gives it to a mercenary changing his status to that of cleruch.

30. The documents quoted are *P. Lille* 4 = *W. Chr.* 336, lines 26–7; *P. Lond.* 2015; and *P. Petrie* III 12 and 14.

31. A minor figures in the document of note 32. On daughters, the prime document is *SB* 9790, of *c.*50 BC: 'To Alexandros, strategos of the Kōite nome, from Rhodokleia daughter of Menippos, orphan, of [the village of] Phebikhis. After the death of my aforementioned father, in accordance with the decrees of our supreme kings, I was certified by the cavalry officer in possession of the twenty arouras of the *klēros* near Molothis left by my father, because there is no male issue.'

32. The papyrus of 142 BC is *P. Med. Bar.* 1, published in *Aegyptus*, 63 (1983), 5.

33. Women: *P. Teb.* 1001 (cf. F. Uebel, *Die Kleruchen Aegyptens . . .* [*Abh. deutschen Akad. Wiss.*, East Berlin, 1968], 41 n. 2). Amnesty: *P. Teb.* 124 = *C. Ord. Ptol.* 54, lines 30–3. Cessions: *BGU* 1261 = 1734; *P. Teb.* 30, 31, 239. A detailed discussion of the formal and legal aspects of the cessions is provided by H.-A. Rupprecht, *Gedächtnisschrift für Wolfgang Kunkel* (Frankfurt, 1984), 365–90.

34. *P. Petrie* III 20 = *W. Chr.* 450, and *P. Teb.* 820. On crown farmers see also note 20, above.

35. The quotations are from *P. Par.* 63 = *UPZ* 110, of 164 BC. For the Roman ultimatum we have the dramatic account of the contemporary historian Polybios (*Histories* Book 29, chapter 27):

> Popillius Laenas, the Roman envoy, handed Antiochos the senate's decree ordering him to end his war against Ptolemy at once and withdraw his army into Syria within a stated time. The king read it and said he wanted to consult his friends about this new development. Whereupon Popillius did something peremptory and exceedingly arrogant, to all appearances. He was carrying a stick cut from a vine. With it he drew a circle around Antiochos and bade him give his reply to the communication right in that circle. The king was taken aback at this high-handed action, but after hesitating a little he said he would do everything required of him by the Romans.

The Romans, Polybios explains further, were fresh from the battle in which they had crushed the third of the great Hellenistic powers, Macedon; 'had this not been so and Antiochos fully aware of it, I do not think he would have obeyed the Romans' orders'.

CHAPTER 2

1. The letters are *P. Petrie* II 16 and 11(1), reprinted as Nos. 4 and 3 in S. Witkowski, *Epistulae Privatae Gracae . . .* , second edn. (Leipzig, 1911). Arsinoē was the sister and wife of Ptolemy II Philadelphos. Together the king and queen were worshipped as the 'sibling gods' (p.161). After her death in 270 BC, many more divine honours were added to enhance the memory and cult of Arsinoē, including her identification with Aphroditē (for the Greeks) and Isis (for the Egyptians). The queens of succeeding Ptolemies were divinized in similar fashion.

2. In the same vein, there is a contemporary instance in the Zenon archive of a Greek working for an Egyptian boatbuilder: *P. Cairo Zenon* 59782(a), line 65.

3. The calculations are paraphrased from those of T. Reekmans, *Archiv für Papyrusforschung*, 20 (1970), 17–24.

4. *P. Petrie* III 43(2), Recto ii. The last sentence is conflated from another such contract of the same year, *P. Petrie* III 43(2), Recto iv. On the dating formula see p. 136. A *schoinion* measured a hundred cubits in length, equivalent to about 52.5 metres.

5. *P. Petrie* II 9(1) and 4(11). An *aōilion* was a measure of volume, equivalent to about half a cubic metre.

6. It was in remote Pharaonic times that workers hit upon the ultimate recourse of fleeing to a sacred precinct, where they would find physical safety in the inviolability of the sanctuary while dramatizing the grievance or grievances that had caused them to abandon their work. The practice continued all through the centuries. Papyri contemporary with those of the Kleon archive tell us of strikes by peasants on the estate of Apollonios (whom we shall meet in the next paragraph), of a flight by quarrymen, and of a group threatening to flee because their pay was late: *P. Cairo Zenon* 59245, *PSI* 421 and 502, *P. Hib.* 71. The most recent study of the subject is that of H. Cadell, *Journ. Econ. Soc. Hist. Orient*, 26 (1983), 22–32.

7. It was Apollonios' (or the king's) idea to develop the estate as a 'model farm', an example which, it was hoped, would stimulate the cleruchs also to engage in undertakings that would expand agricultural production, to the benefit of the country's economy as a whole. (This was most noticeable, probably, in the cultivation of the grape, which, while not unknown in pre-Ptolemaic Egypt, was now expanded by the immigrants' consumption of wine to the status of a major crop.) The papyri bear witness to such activities on the estate as the opening of new farmland through the clearing of brush and the spread of the irrigation system, and we read of attempts, some successful, some not, to acclimatize non-native flora, both Greek and exotic. A centre for every kind of agricultural and related activity, Apollonios' estate also acted as a lodestone, attracting to newly founded Philadelphia both Greeks who saw good business opportunities there, and Egyptians who seized at the opportunities afforded for employment in farming and the manual trades.

8. The letters are *P. Petrie* II 13(5) (= *P. L. Bat.* XX Suppl. C); 4(8) (= III 42 *c* 1); and 13(1). For Diotimos see p. 41 above. The name Dionysios is too common for a sure identification, but it is likely that the man mentioned here was either Apollonios' agent of that name residing in the Memphite nome (which adjoined Philadelphia on the east), or the nome financial officer.

9. *P. Petrie* II 42 H 8(f) = Witkowski, op. cit., No. 6.

10. *P. Petrie* II 13(19) = *P. Lond.* 945 = *Select Papyri* 94. The Nile was normally at it lowest levels from April to mid-June.

11. *P. Petrie* II 42(a).

CHAPTER 3

1. J. Bingen, *Proc. Twelfth International Congr. Papyrology* [*Amer. Stud. in Papyrology* 7, 1970], 36–7, 40. On the Egyptian workers' strike weapon, see Chapter 2, note 6.

2. The private bank is mentioned in *P. Oxy.* 1639, which dates from either 73 or 44 BC.

3. The 1981 study is that of R. Bogaert in *L'Antiquité classique*, 50 (1981), 86–99, where references to earlier bibliography will also be found.

4. *P. Grad.* 4. Sibling gods: Chapter 1, note 2. Benefactor gods: Ptolemy III Euergetēs ('benefactor') and his queen, Berenikē. Flight for sanctuary: Chapter 2, note 6.

5. The papyri are quoted in the following order: *P. Hamb.* 171, 172, 169, 170, 177, 176, 173.

6. Records of papyrus rolls used by Apollonios' clerks appear in *P. Cairo Zenon* 59687 and *P. Col. Zenon* 4.

7. From here to the end of the chapter documents from the Zenon archive are quoted in the following order: *P. Cairo Zenon* 59022; *P. Wis.* 77 = *SB* 6797; *P. Col. Zenon* 45; *P. Lond.* 1938; *P. Cairo Zenon* 59253, 59504, 59470; *PSI* 363, 333.

CHAPTER 4

1. H. Bengtson, *Die Strategie in der hellenistischen Zeit* III (= *Münchener Beiträge* . . . , 36 [1952]), 13.

2. The one instance is *P. Ent.* 82 = *Select Papyri* 269.

3. *P. Ent.* 11, 86, and 79. In No. 86 Diophanes' instruction is lost to us in the fragmentary state of the papyrus; the date, written in a notation (also incompletely preserved) on the back, corresponds to 26 or 27 February 221 BC. In No. 79, Diophanes' instruction was not recorded; the date, noted on the back, corresponds to 11 May 218 BC.

Among the ordinances of Alexandria preserved for us on a papyrus of *c*.250 BC is the following (*P. Hal.* 1, lines 203–9):

'In re: blows between free men. If a free man or free woman aggressor with unjust hands strikes a free man or free woman, there shall be a uniform penalty of 100 drachmas upon conviction. If he/she strikes more than one blow, the plaintiff shall present in court his/her own claim of damages for the blows, and the defendant shall pay twice the amount awarded by the court. If anyone strikes any of the magistrates performing the duties that that magistracy is charged with performing, he/she shall upon conviction pay the prescribed penalty threefold.'

No similar evidence is at hand for the rest of the country outside Alexandria, but doubtless provisions of a similar nature applied.

4. *P. Ent.* 60.
5. *P. Ent.* 28, 32, and 89.
6. *UPZ* 124.
7. *P. Ent.* 47, 44, and 66. The ninety-nine-year lease, so common in English and American law, occurs very infrequently in documents from Hellenistic times. That may be because the vast majority of extant leases relate to farmland, where leases for one or a few years were the rule. It is understandable, however, that in the case of a building lot, a lessee would want some assurance of at least semi-permanence before engaging to erect a structure on the site.
8. *P. Ent.* 49 and 25. In the first of these, Sopolis' reference to his services to the kings presumably identifies him as a mercenary soldier or cleruch. There is in this petition, it will have been noticed, no request for referral of the matter, and no instruction, to a village police chief. That is because the accused lives in the nome capital. Since this is where the strategos also resides and has his office, the petitioner asks that the strategos himself handle the matter. This he does, as the notation indicates, by assigning it to a deputy.

   In connection with the second of these petitions it is worth noting that in another papyrus in the Diophanes archive an aged father complains of neglect by an ungrateful daughter: *P. Ent.* 26 = *Select Papyri* 268.
9. The first of these reports is *P. Sorbonne* inv. no. 2410, published in *Livre du centenaire de l'Institut français d'archéologie orientale* (Cairo, 1980), 309. In the second, published as *P. Turner* 16, the description of the seal employed was included to enable the recipient to verify that this official report had not been opened (which would involve breaking the seal) and the information in it altered while *en route* from the village to the strategos' office. (Inv. no. 2410 is now reprinted as *SB* 12426.)

CHAPTER 5

1. Serapeum, the Latinized spelling of the word, has generally been used in the past. For the more recent practice, retaining the original Greek form of names, see the Prefatory Notes.
2. *UPZ* 106.
3. M. J. Price and B. L. Trell, *Coins and their Cities* (London and Detroit, 1977), 183.
4. *P. Oxy.* 1381 (lines 61–278).

5. The quotation is from *Iliad*, Book 1, verse 63.
6. The 'troubles' in which Glaukias lost his life will appear in Chapter 6.
7. *UPZ* 14.
8. For more detail on these matters see D. J. (Thompson) Crawford, *Studia Hellenistica*, 24 (1980), 5–42.
9. The two drafts, dating from 163 BC, are *UPZ* 18 and 19.
10. The dreams are collected in *UPZ* 77–80. The italicized words in the next-to-last selection are probably nonsense syllables. They are not Greek; if they are intended to represent anything in the Egyptian language, they are so corrupted that no one has yet succeeded in deciphering them.

    Ammon, identified with Zeus in one of his manifestations, was the earliest Greek god established in Egypt; his famous oracular shrine at the Siwa oasis in the western desert dates from at least the sixth and possibly the seventh century BC. Anubis was an Egyptian funerary god represented in the form of a big black dog.
11. The papyri quoted are *UPZ* 7, 8, and 15. The revolt mentioned in the first document, put down only a year or two before, was the one in which Ptolemaios' father lost his life: see Chapter 6.

CHAPTER 6

1. For data on life expectancy, see, most recently, N. Lewis, *Life in Egypt under Roman Rule* (Oxford, 1983), 54.
2. The problem of the marriage with Sarapias is discussed in N. Lewis, *Chronique d'Égypte*, 57 (1982), 317–18. If Sarapias was Dryton's second wife and Esthladas was born in the first years of their marriage, the date of the relevant will was presumably 156/5, miswritten 176/5 by a scribe's *lapsus calami*. The documents containing Dryton's wills are listed in note 12, below.
3. The priest of Pathyris and Krokodilopolis appears in *P. Lond.* 889a (*c.*137 BC). Several of the Demotic documents will be referred to or quoted later in this chapter.
4. On the exposure of neonates by the Greek immigrants to Egypt and their descendants see the reference in note 1, above.
5. For Esthladas' property see *P. Lond.* 889a and the end of this chapter.
6. The document is *P. Grenf.* I 20. At the time of this loan the ratio of copper to silver drachmas was about 500:1.
7. The revelation of the true meaning of 'free of interest' was made by P. W. Pestman in *Journal of Juristic Papyrology*, 16–17 (1971), 7–29. The loan quoted is *P. Grenf.* I 18.
8. The contrary view, i.e. that there were two different women named Heraïs/Tisris, is held by R. K. Ritner, *Grammatika Demotika (Festschrift für Erich Lüddeckens)* (Würzburg, 1984), 178–9.
9. *P. Bad. Dem.* VI.
10. For Esthladas' wife see *Chronique d'Égypte*, 57 (1982), 320–1.
11. *W. Chr.* 10 = *Select Papyri* 101.

12. The first will is known only from a reference to it in the third. The second will is preserved in *SB* 4637 + *P. Grenf.* I 12; *P. Bad.* II 5 is an exiguous fragment of another copy. A nearly complete text of the third will is *P. Grenf.* I 21 = *M. Chr.* 302 = *Select Papyri* 83, which is quoted three paragraphs below; fragments of a second copy are *P. Grenf.* I 44 + *P. Bour.* 9 = *P. Lugd.-Bat.* XIX 4.

13. P. W. Pestman, *P. Lugd.-Bat.* XIX, p. 36, n. 16, wonders whether Dryton was compelled to resort to witnesses signing in Demotic because he and his family were 'boycotted' by the other Greeks of Pathyris in reprisal for their Egyptianizing way of life—an intriguing notion, but one which, in the present state of the evidence, must remain purely speculative and, indeed, rather dubious: see further note 16, below.

14. *P. Grenf.* I 21 = *M. Chr.* 302 = *Select Papyri* 83. See also note 2, above.

15. *P. Lond.* 401 = *M. Chr.* 18.

16. The documents referred to are *P. Grenf.* II 26 and *WO* 1617 and 1618. Studies of immigrant populations in modern times reveal that women are usually quicker than men to conform to the ways of their new environment.

The conclusion (op. cit., note 8 above, 187) of R. K. Ritner's publication of the Chicago Demotic papyrus constitutes an apt ending to the present chapter:

> The papyri of the families of Hermocrates and Dryton provide an unparalleled view of the Egyptianization of Greek colonists under the Ptolemies. The genealogical revisions made possible by [this] papyrus indicate the early date of the assimilation, as the first attested generation of the family already bears a double name (Apollonios/Nakhtor). . . . [Nor is] the reverse process documented [here]—the Hellenization of Egyptians. Rather, the stated Cyrenaic and Cretan designations of Apollonia *et al.* and Dryton, respectively, should be taken seriously, and the family's use of Demotic legal instruments is all the more striking. The provincial setting of Pathyris, subject to political instabilities and lacking in Greek speakers, must be largely responsible.

CHAPTER 7

1. *The Tebtunis Papyri*, I, v–vii.

2. *P. Teb.* 10 = *Select Papyri* 339.

3. The decrees quoted are found in *P. Teb.* 5 = *Select Papyri* 210 = *C. Ord. Ptol.* 53, lines 93–8 and 162–7.

4. Menkhes' bid is contained in *P. Teb.* 9.

5. Hereditary leases are mentioned in one of the decrees of 118 BC: above, note 3, lines 10–13. The troubled half-dozen years before 164 BC saw Antiochos IV of Syria invade and proclaim himself king of Egypt, until Roman intervention forced him to betake himself and his army home again in ignominious retreat. The story, which became an almost legendary, much-repeated anecdote in antiquity, is quoted in note 35 of

Chapter 1. After Antiochos' forced withdrawal Egypt was still riven for years by a struggle for the throne between Ptolemy VI and his younger brother. That dispute too was settled, at least temporarily, by the Romans. The brother outlived Ptolemy VI and craftily managed to succeed him on the throne (p. 107).

6. The parcels of land referred to are recorded in, respectively, *P. Teb.* 75 (lines 30–1), 65 (lines 17–23) = 75 (lines 50–1), 75 (lines 3–14), 107, and 164 (line 12).

7. D. J. (Thompson) Crawford, *Kerkeosiris, an Egyptian Village in the Ptolemaic Period* (Cambridge, 1971), 4.

8. The examples are *P. Teb.* 84, lines 49–57, and 87, lines 49–51. The 'excess' of $17/32$ arouras is the difference between the area of 8 arouras arrived at by calculation and the total of $7^{15}/32$ resulting from the on-the-spot survey. A *schoinion* was a hundred cubits in length, i.e. about 52.5 metres.

9. The documents referred to are *P. Teb.* 63 and 91. The example quoted is *P. Teb.* 74, lines 1–30. Examination of the details of this last passage reveals that Menkhes occasionally made small errors in adding up fractions—errors of the order of $1/48$ to $3/4$.

10. *P. Teb.* 71.

11. *P. Teb.* 67. The ratio of wheat to barley was 3:5. Olyra was an ancient variety of triticum. Here too Menkhes' addition contains errors.

12. *P. Teb.* 27, 26, and 5 (= *Select Papyri* 210 = *C. Ord. Ptol.* 53), lines 83–4. Strikes and asylum figure also above, pp. 42, 47, 50.

13. *P. Teb.* 43.

14. The population estimate is that of D. J. Crawford, op. cit. (above, note 7), 124. A papyrus in Florence, published in 1983, gives evidence of a Jewish community in the Arsinoite village of Philadelphia: *PSI XVII Congr.* 22.

15. The document is *P. Teb.* 14, of 114 BC.

16. The document is *P. Teb.* 24.

17. *P. Teb.* 38 (the earlier complaint is 39). The procedure for handling such complaints had obviously changed or broadened from that of a century earlier, as we saw it in Chapter 4 (where they were submitted to the nome strategos, who instructed the village police chief to act in the matter).

18. *P. Teb.* 49. The date stated in the second sentence corresponds to 8 November 113.

19. *P. Teb.* 46; the four other complaints against the same marauders are Nos. 45, 47, 126, and 127. The attacks occurred on 23 August 113.

20. *P. Teb.* 53. The date of the incident corresponds to 9 October 110.

21. The attribution of the writing to Polemon's successor is made by P. W. Pestman, *Festschrift . . . Papyrus Erzherzog Rainer* (Vienna, 1983), 129.

CHAPTER 8

1. The contracts are *PLB* 17, 19, and 20 = *P. Rein.* 20, 23, 24, and Demotic

3. The royal edict is *P. Teb.* 5 = *C. Ord. Ptol.* 53, lines 207–17; although it was published at the beginning of this century and has been the subject of much commentary since then, its precise meaning was only recently established by J. Modrzejewski, *Le Monde grec: hommages à Claire Préaux* (Brussels, 1975), 707.

2. The text that follows is *PLB* 11 = *P. Rein.* 18. Dionysios' borrowings and the uses to which he could have put them are discussed in *Bulletin of the American Society of Papyrologists*, 20 (1983), 55–8.

3. *P. Teb.* 5 = *Select Papyri* 210 = *C. Ord. Ptol.* 53, lines 221–6.

4. *PLB* 35 = *P. Rein.* 11.

5. *PLB* 10 = *P. Rein.* 17. The last sentence of the complaint, where the papyrus is fragmented, obviously ended with one of the standard formulas, e.g. 'I will have obtained justice'. See the numerous examples in Chapter 4.

   The border of the Kynopolite nome lay some thirty kilometres north of Akoris. Sotionkhis was probably Paësis' wife.

6. *PLB* 7. On the dating formula with which the contract opens, see the next note. Ammonopolis was obviously somewhere in the vicinity, but its precise location is unknown to us.

7. Up to this point, after naming the ruling king and queen, the formula refers to the priests of the cults of Alexander the Great, of Ptolemies I–V with their queens, then of Ptolemies VII, VI, VII and VIII, and of the currently reigning Ptolemy IX with his queen. In the rest of the formula after Isis come the queens of Ptolemies VIII, III, VIII, II, VIII, IV. Some of the Greek epithets are translated in the Demotic version, which follows immediately after this Greek document. All the epithets are translated in the Prefatory Notes.

   Audnaios and Lōïos were months in the Macedonian calendar: cf. the Prefatory Notes for further details on the calendar.

8. This penalty is several times the market price, especially at harvest time, when the supply was at its peak and the price at its lowest.

9. It is interesting to see how the Demotic renders the Greek *eupatōr*, which really means 'born of a noble father'.

10. The documents quoted are *PLB* 17 and 3 (Demotic). The Egyptian god Thōt(h) was the tutelary divinity of the nome, which was called Hermopolite in Greek as a result of the equation of Thot(h) with Hermes.

11. The descriptions of Totoēs and Takmeïs are found in *P. Strassb.* 84 and 85, of 114 and 113 BC. The physical characteristics of the parents were reproduced in the daughters, one of them short, the other of medium height.

12. The Totoēs documents are *P. Strassb. Dem.* 21; *P. Strassb.* 85; *P. Grenf.* II 18; *P. Lond.* 880 and 1203. The sale by the daughters to Panebkhounis' wife is *P. Lond.* 1204.

13. The Takmeïs documents are, in the order cited, *P. Grenf.* II 17, 16 (= *M. Chr.* 138, 137), and 18; *P. Strassb.* 83 and 84. The text of this last, in which her physical appearance is recorded, is given below (p. 150).

14. The tax receipts are, in chronological order, *BGU* 1434; *WO* 1620; *SB*

9553 (3); *P. Strassb.* 82; Matha *Dem. O.* 113 and 228–30.

15. The contracts, in the order cited, are *P. Lond.* 1203, 10500 (Demotic) and 879; *M. Chr.* 233; *P. Strassb.* 87; *P. Lips.* 7.
16. The documents are *P. Adler Dem.* 9 and *P. Lond.* 1206.
17. The documents are cited in the following order: *P. Strassb.* 87; *P. Lond.* 1206; *P. Strassb.* 85.
18. *P. Strassb.* 84. The specification that this was river-bank land is made to distinguish it from land in less desirable locations, such as on islands in the river, whose contours were constantly being altered by the flow of the Nile. The signature at the end is 'Herakleides, banker' in abbreviated form.
19. *BGU* 994.
20. *P. Grenf.* II 23a = *Select Papyri* 27.
21. The documents referred to in this paragraph are, in the order cited, *P. Grenf.* II 26, 27 and 30 (lines 7–11 and 27–9); *BGU* 1260; *P. Grenf.* II 28.
22. *P. Strassb. Dem.* 43 = E. Lüddeckens, *Eheverträge* 45.

EPILOGUE

1. The houseboat is described in Athenaios' *The Learned Banqueters*, Book 5, chapter 37.
2. The reference is to Plutarch's *Life of Mark Antony*, chapter 27.

MAPS

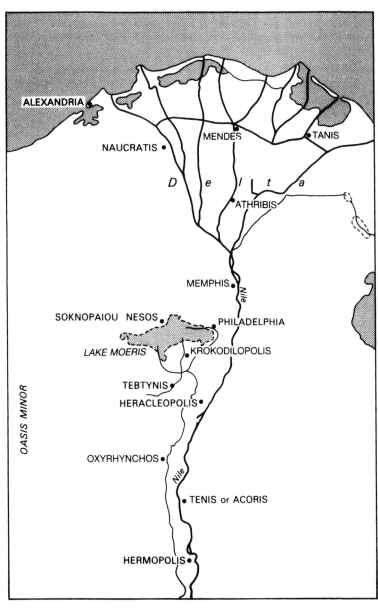

Map 1. Ptolemaic Egypt

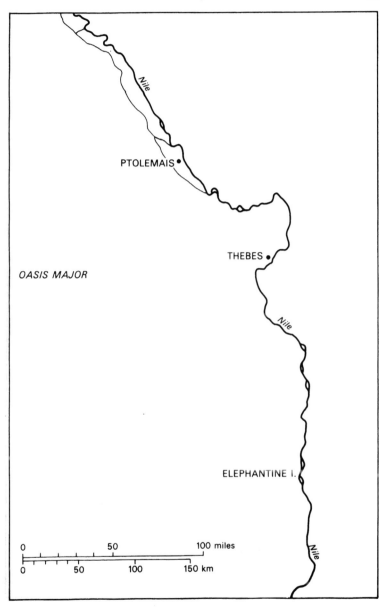

Maps

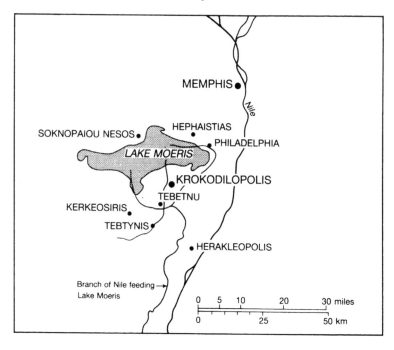

Map 2. Arsinoite nome and vicinity

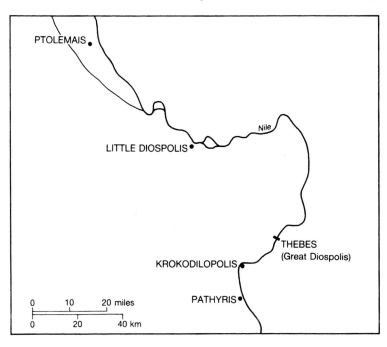

Map 3. Ptolemais to Pathyris

Description of Plates

1. (*a*) This reverse (enlarged) of a coin issued by the mint of Alexandria in the late second century AD shows a ship sailing past the Pharos as it enters the harbour (Chapter 1). In contrast to most of the reconstructions of the edifice which were proposed in the nineteenth and the first half of the twentieth century— 'more or less fantasies', in the words of one recent writer—the true form of the Pharos is depicted on this and similar coins. Its total height was about 120 metres. The lower part tapered as it rose from a base revealed by the ruins to have been a square with sides some 31 metres (100 feet) long. The figures at the top of that section were tritons puffing on conch shells; one recent theory holds that they served as foghorns when compressed air was passed through them. Who was represented by the bronze statue at the very top of the tower, whether god or human, is much disputed by scholars, but it is probable that the statue, in addition to being honorific, served as a reflector for the flame of the guiding light. (Photograph courtesy of The American Numismatic Society).

(*b*) This miniature bronze statuette of Aphrodite dressing her hair, which formed the head of a hairpin, was one of over a hundred bronze objects found at Galjub just north of Cairo in the early part of this century. The objects were apparently display samples of wares that customers could order from a metal-workers' shop. About 250 BC. (Hildesheim, Pelizaeus-Museum 2273).

2. (*a*) A painted sign found in the ruins of the Serapeion at Memphis (Chapter 5). The Greek legend reads in translation: 'I interpret dreams under commission of the god. With good fortune! The interpreter of these things is a Cretan.' The sign, in the form of a temple facade, has a Greek pediment and roof supported by naked Egyptian goddesses—a structural hybridization in keeping with the hybrid divinity of the god Serapis. Beneath the Greek legend are an altar and an Apis bull. (Cairo Museum).

(*b*) Dozens of painted grave stelae of Ptolemaic date have been found near Alexandria, many of them like this one, with pediment above and pillars at the sides to simulate a small chapel. The painted inscription says, 'Dionysios, from Bithynia, farewell'. The deceased, shown at the left, was obviously a soldier: he holds a long spear, wears what appear to be military boots, and is accompanied by his boy-attendant who carries two shorter spears and his master's shield. Third century BC. (Alexandria Museum).

3. (*a*) In this memorandum (third century BC) the writer complains that one of the irrigation channels has been overflowing and endangering the pigs and other farm animals. At the bottom he has drawn a diagram showing the course of the canal and the emplacement of a semi-circular palisade that he proposes should be erected to protect the animals. (Campbell Cowan Edgar, *Zenon Papyri in the University of Michigan*, Ann Arbor 1931, Plate VI).

(*b*) This is a copy, in the elegant calligraphy of the period, of an order issued by Ptolemy III Euergetes in March/April of 237 BC. The two words at the head of the document are the standard opening of such promulgations, 'By order of the king'. The text of this order relates to sureties in lawsuits. (Ibid., Plate IV).

4. Greek techniques began to influence Egyptian art even before the conquest by Alexander the Great and the ensuing waves of Greek immigration. On the walls of the tomb of Petosiris, an Egyptian priest of the fourth century BC, the scenes of everyday life, traditional in Egyptian funerary art since early Pharaonic times, are modified according to Greek styles and canons, especially in composition and in the depiction of movement, faces, hair, and clothes. (Photograph: Hirmer Fotoarchiv).

5. The south wall of the peristyle of a sumptuous tomb discovered near Alexandria in the early 1930s. Except for the rather piquant addition of the Egyptian-inspired sphinxes flanking the brightly polychromed doorways, the entire structure conforms to Greek styles and traditions in its ornamental as well as architectural details. Above the central

doorway is a mural executed at least partly in fresco. It shows three riders in the garb of Macedonian cavalrymen alternating with two female figures. All five, with sacral objects in their hands, appear to be partaking in a ceremony, presumably funeral or memorial rites for the family members entombed here, performed at the altar between the central cavalryman and the priestess to his right. The figures and costumes are depicted in bright colours—violet, brown, red, yellow, pink and blue—against a sky-blue background. Late third or early second century BC. (Alexandria: *Annuaire du Musée Greco-romain* 1934–5, Plato XXVII).

6. (*a*) A clay head of a Ptolemaic queen of the third century BC, probably Arsinoē II or Berenikē II (consorts of Ptolemy II and III, respectively). The diadem and earrings were covered with a yellow glaze to simulate gold. Except for her place of residence there is nothing Egyptian about this queen. (Photograph courtesy of the Trustees of the British Museum).

(*b*) In this granite statue of the late second century BC a Ptolemaic queen appears in the form and trappings of the goddess Isis (Chapter 8). The most striking quality of the many such statues and statuettes that have been found is their inharmonious juxtaposition, a clash rather than a blending, of Egyptian and Greek sculptural traditions. Cf. Plate 5. (Yale University Art Gallery; purchased from Mrs Mabel Scott).

7. Representing themselves to the native population as legitimate continuators of the line of Pharaohs, the Ptolemies erected temples such as this in the traditional Egyptian style, and had themselves depicted on the walls in the garb and performing the traditional worship of the Pharaohs. This very large temple at Edfu, almost completely preserved, was erected under Ptolemy III Euergetes. (Photograph courtesy of the Griffith Institute, Oxford).

8. This scene appears on the rear wall of the Temple of Hathor at Dendera (ancient Tentyra), just north of Thebes. Cf. Plate 7. (Photograph Martin R. Davies).

Index

Addenda et Corrigenda

Page	Line	
89	17	Sarapias (not Sarapias')
92	8-9	In the light of a fragment published by W. Clarysse in *Chronique d'Égypte* 61 (1986) 99-103, this sentence should now read as follows: "Dryton was transferred to Pathyris *c.* 152 BC, remarried at Latopolis (the bride's home town presumably) in 150, and resided at Pathyris for the rest of his life."
99	1-2	This sentence should now read as follows: "Of the first, drawn up in 176/5 BC, there are some very small fragments, identified in 1987, in Florence."
101	20	In the light of R. Scholl, *Chronique d'Égypte* 63 (1988) 141-44, who dates Dryton's death between 126 and 123/2 BC, "some fifteen years later" should be changed to "not long after."
101	29	Delete the words "not long."
139	22	In the light of J. Bingen, *Chronique d'Égypte* 64 (1989) 235 and note 3, this should now read: "twenty-one of them Demotic, fifty-three Greek and two bilingual."
168	n. 10	Add: "The modern reader cannot fail to be struck by the symbolism—cultural, psychological, sexual—in many of the dreams."
169	n. 12	Replace the first sentence with the following: "The fragments of the first will were identified by Gabriella Messeri and published by her in *Papyrologica Florentina* 19 (1990) 429-36. Prior to that, our only knowledge of the first will was a reference to it in the third will."
170	n. 14	Add: "*P. Münch.* 49, published in 1986, a letter of the second century BC to the presbyteroi of the Jews of Tebetnoi, attests the existence of a Jewish community also in the Herakleopolite nome."

Reviews

Antiquité Classique 58 (1989) 430-31 (Alain Martin)
Bibliotheca Orientalis 45 (1988) col. 137-139 (Claude Orrieux)
Boletin del Seminario de Estudios de Arte y Arqueologia 53 (1987) 474 (Balil)
Choice (May 1997) 91-92 (Peter Green)
Classical Review n.s. 37 (1987) 247-48 (Dominic Rathbone)
Classical World 82 (1988) 132-33 (Jerry Clack)
Greece and Rome 34 (1987) 221-22 (Susan M. Sherwin-White)
Gymnasium 96 (1989) 247-48 (Konrad Kinzl)
Hermathena 144 (1988) 114-20 (Brian McGing)
Journal of Ecclesiastical History 38 (1987) 410 (P. M. Fraser)
Journal of Hellenic Studies 108 (1988) 253-54 (Dorothy J. Thompson)
Les Études Classiques 57 (1989) 85 (Jean Straus)
New England Classical Newsletter 16 (1988) 38-39 (Jan Gabbert)
Revue Historique de Droit Français et Étranger 67 (1989) 507 (J. Modrzejewski), repr. *Journal of Juristic Papyrology* 21 (1991) 109
Times Literary Supplement 86 (1987) 640 (J. D. Ray)

1. (a) (*Above*) A ship sailing past the
Pharos of Alexandria

(b) (*Right*) A bronze statuette of
Aphrodite

3. (a) An irrigation problem (b) A royal decree

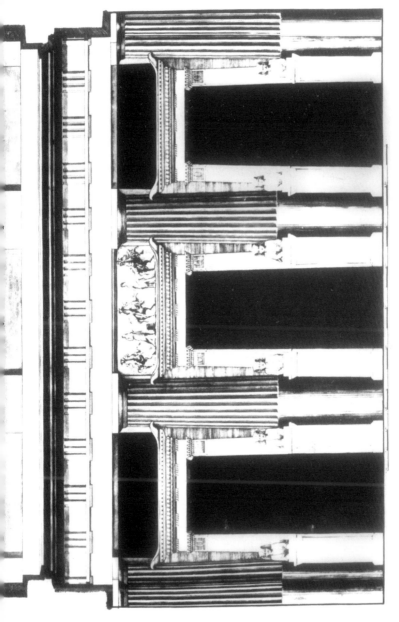

5. A tomb near Alexandria: South wall of the peristyle

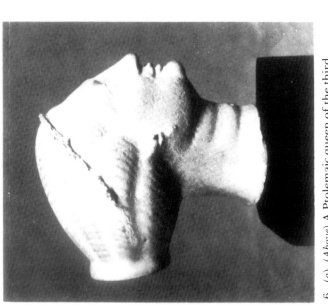

6. (a) (*Above*) A Ptolemaic queen of the third century BC

(b) (*Right*) A Ptolemaic queen of the second century BC represented as the goddess Isis

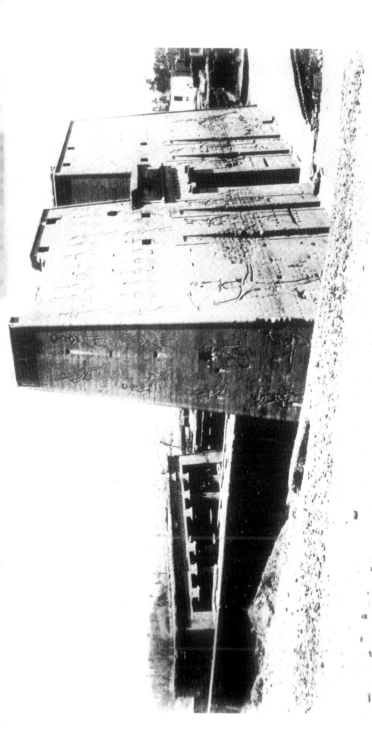

7. Temple of Horus at Edfu: Front pylon

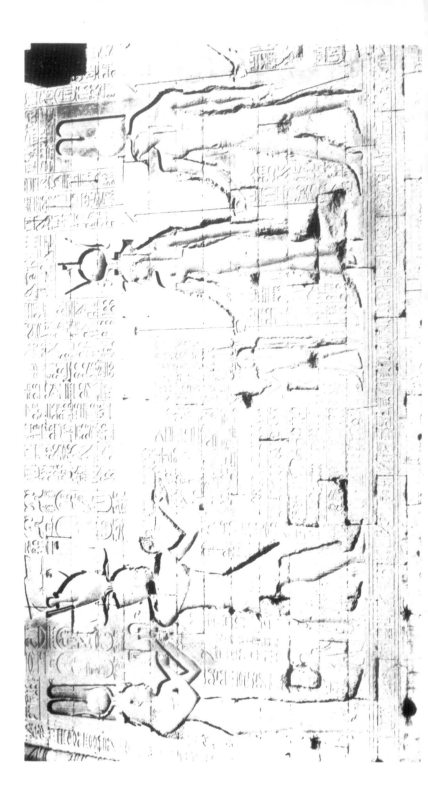